THE LIFE OF ST. ULRICH OF AUGSBURG

THE LIFE OF ST. ULRICH OF AUGSBURG

GERHARD OF AUGSBURG

Copyright 2024 by Dalcassian Press

All rights reserved. No part of this book may be reproduced in any manner whatsoever without written permission except in the case of brief quotations embodied in critical articles and reviews.

No part of this publication may be reproduced, distributed, or transmitted in any form or by any means, including photocopying, recording, or other electronic or mechanical methods, without the prior written permission of the publisher, except in the case of brief quotations embodied in critical reviews and certain other non-commercial uses permitted by copyright law. For permission requests, write to Dalcassian Press at admin@thescriptoriumproject.com

Translator: Curtin, D.P. (1985-)

ISBN: 979-8-3483-0129-3 (Paperback)
ISBN: 979-8-3483-0130-9 (eBook)
Library of Congress Control Number:

Printed by Ingram Content Group, 1 Ingram Blvd, La Vergne, Tennessee
First Printing 2024, Dalcassian Press, Wilmington, DE

This work is part of a series produced in association with the Scriptorium Project and its community of scholars and translators.
Please visit our website at: www.thescriptoriumproject.com

THE LIFE OF ST. ULRICH OF AUGSBURG

Many were frequently knocking with the fame of the miracles of Christ, which he granted to be done through his servant, the holy Ulrich, in honor of his most holy mother, Mary, and still their minds were occupied with doubt. They sent legates to me wishing to know the truths of things from my responses, asking me to make clear to them what I could have known in truth with a lucid description. And when such a multitude of questioners surrounded me with inquiries from all sides, so that I deemed it impossible to give written answers to each individually, I began to think silently within myself, that since I had sought to experience the origin of his birth with quiet experience, I could, having described his origin, make the subsequent life and death common to all who were questioning and wishing to read, not trusting in my preceding merits, nor in the sharpness of my mind, but hoping in the mercy of Almighty God, who said: "Open your mouth, and I will fill it;" so that through the merits of the aforementioned bishop, by the irrigation of the Holy Spirit and the fervor of divine fire, He might deign to direct my understanding, that what He inspired me to think, He would not withdraw the strength to accomplish, unless He granted me to publish it with a suitable measure predetermined in my mind, so that those who love God might have examples of edification before them, and for those despising the commandments of God, might increase the benefit of conversion or the threat of damnation. We confidently trust in the love of Christ for those reading this, that the help of Almighty God may be present, so that through His servant they may be supported in this world, and with His assistance may be brought to eternal joys.

First of all, we must not remain silent about the interpretation of the name of such a great man, with the help of the Holy Spirit. Therefore, in the Theutonic language, the inheritance left by the ancestors is called Altuodal, Ric signifies riches, therefore Vodalricus can be interpreted as rich from paternal inheritance, for he flourished enriched by the inheritance of the eternal Father, about whom we say daily in our prayer: "Our Father, who art in heaven," etc. To whose inheritance, Saint Paul comforts those persevering in the will of God, saying: "Indeed, heirs of God, and co-heirs of Christ" (Rom. VIII; I Cor. II); concerning which inheritance it is also written: "What eye has not seen, nor ear heard, nor has ascended in the heart of man, what God has prepared for those who love Him" (I Cor. II); the summary of which not only enjoys itself but also draws many in various ways with the consolations of benefits in this pilgrimage, and will introduce them in various helps and continuous miracles, as is found in the following.

I. Therefore, of blessed memory, Saint Ulrich, born of the noble lineage of the Alemanni from religious and noble parents, namely father Hupald and mother Thetpirga, who, being nursed in the usual manner and raised with utmost care, although having an elegant stature, was so emaciated that it would have been a source of shame for his caregivers if anyone unknown had seen his face. Indeed, as his father and mother marveled why he was afflicted with such frailty and deformity of body, and often thought about it, during the twelfth week after his birth, a certain unknown cleric, arriving by chance, begged to be received by them for a few days in hospitality; who, being kindly received, while sitting with them in the courtyard of their house during the meal, heard a little child crying in the chamber, and inquired whose child it was. Out of shame for the child's emaciation, and with them unwilling to indicate, he said: "If you wish him to be safe, he must be weaned quickly." They, disregarding his words, did not withdraw him from nursing. The next day, hearing him cry again, he said: "Why did you not act according to my advice?" They, still contemptuous of his counsel, did not believe him. On the third day, hearing the child's cry weaker than before, he said to them: "Because of your negligence, this little one is being handed over to destruction; know for sure that if he is not withdrawn from the breasts, he will die this night; but if withdrawn, he will be saved; in the future, something great will be manifested in him by the Lord." Then at last, obeying him, they began to sustain him with other foods. He was immediately revived, progressing day by day, and received such a form of beauty that his own parents looked upon him with joy and showed him to others. They praised the Lord day and night for the safety of the child, and for the fact that he had sent them such a guest who understood the discretion of this matter. Therefore, believing in the future from the past, they considered where they might find a most religious and most studious life of teaching, and having taken counsel, they commended him to the monastery of Saint Gall, because there was a multitude of noble servants of God, and the devotion to learning and teaching was held at that time. He was entrusted to a certain religious man skilled in the art of grammar, named Waning, from whom he received well the daily teaching of religion and reading, and he implanted it in the depths of his heart, so much so that little by little the brothers felt him progressing exceedingly in the fruits of doctrine, and for this reason they endeavored to take him into the fellowship of their brotherhood. Often urged by their petitions, he requested a delay in responding. Then, seeking counsel, he approached a certain enclosed woman named Wiberat who was residing there; she, responding, said to him: "Come to me after three days, if it pleases God, you will be able to perceive my counsel." From there, he withdrew, and she fervently prayed to the Lord that on the appointed day she might be able to manifest to him a certain and true indication of counsel. When he had come to receive the answer, she said to him: "Do not let your mind be occupied by hesitation, because the spiritual father of this monastery, decreed by God to govern, you will not establish; but in the eastern part, where a certain river divides two regions, in the future you must serve God in the episcopal ministry, and in the same place you will endure many such laborious things as your predecessors never suffered from pagans and wicked Christians, which, however, with God's help, you will most decently overcome in the end." Having heard this, he revealed it to the most secret brothers, and mitigated their persuasion with sweet conversation, and he set aside all hope of his former destination; and yet, he did not cease his study of learning, but interacted charitably with everyone there; until, in due time, filled with the double nourishment of knowledge and religion, consoled by the common prayer of all, and relying on the love of brotherhood, he lovingly revisited his parents. Then, having taken wise counsel, they placed him under the authority of the bishop of the Church of Augsburg, Adalbero, whom they recognized as filled with much wisdom at that time, endowed with the art of music above others, and arranging nearly all the reins of the kingdom with the king. He, indeed, due to the nobility of his parents, and his good nature and beauty, gladly received him, entrusted him with the ministry of the chamberlain. Having taken this on, and with other benefits according to his dignity, as he was precocious in all things, he prosperously advanced day by day. Meanwhile, it pleased him to visit the thresholds of the blessed apostles Peter and Paul. When he arrived there, he was well received by the venerable Pope Marinus, and when questioned by him about which province or city he was from, he replied: "I am from the province of Alemannia, and from the city of Augusta, and I serve Adalbero, the bishop of the same city." — "Do not be troubled in your mind, brother," he said, "the one of whom you spoke to me, your elder Adalbero, has departed from this world, and, God willing, it is fitting for you to be the pastor of that same church." Indeed, as he hesitated, he said: "Why do you refuse God's destination? If now you refuse to receive it in tranquility, unshaken and undisturbed, in the future you will receive it in destruction and plunder, and you will govern and rebuild it with labor." The next day, without the pope's permission, due to the sadness of his deceased lord, and lest he be further constrained by words from him, he left Rome and returned to Augusta, and found it just as the aforementioned pope had predicted. Then Hiltin became the successor of Adalbero. However, he was not of such high stature that he wished to apply himself to service. Meanwhile, after his father's death, he returned to take care of his mother, remembering the command of the Lord saying: Honor your father and your mother (Exod. XX), etc. Therefore, he diligently cared for her and arranged all her affairs as far as the strength granted to him by the Lord allowed. After fifteen years, when Bishop Hiltin had died, presented to King Heinrich through the machinations of his nephew, Duke Burchard, and other relatives, the death of the bishop was made known to him, and it was requested that the aforementioned lord Ulrich be granted episcopal power by him. The king, observing the nobility of his stature, and discovering the knowledge of his learning, granted their petition, and in royal manner received him into his hands, and honored him with the gift of the pontificate. When these things were thus accomplished, returning with a cheerful spirit from the king, and arriving in Augusta, according to the king's edict, he completed the investiture of the episcopate with the power of his hand. In the course of time, on the feast day of the Nativity of the Lord, according to customary rite, his ordination was carried out. From there, returning home prosperously, and seeing the walls of the church laid low on all sides, and all the buildings too much fallen, as they had been consumed by fire under the former bishop, then greatly troubled in mind, he thought about how he could most suitably rebuild what was so utterly destroyed: because a great part of the household had been killed by pagans, and the towns burned and plundered, while the part of the household that remained was afflicted with great poverty. Nevertheless, having acquired architects and gathered a multitude of the household, he began to restore the ruins with keen insight, and to arrange them quite sensibly, striving with great fervor of spirit that he would not cease to complete what he had begun. And when the man of great sweetness ardently fulfilled the work begun, although pressed by the furniture, relying then on divine aid, he endeavored to adorn all the interiors of that temple with every kind of decoration as much as he could; and also frequently, with keen eyesight, carefully surveying the positions of the church both inside and outside, he complained that the smallness of the dim crypt and its meanness displeased him too much, and he professed that he would place it more appropriately and decently, if God would grant it. When the work seemed to grow sufficiently, it appeared to him in an ecstasy of mind that he ought to chant psalms with a certain brother named Rambert, as was his custom, and in the meantime, he saw Bishop Adalbero, dressed in vestments for mass, appearing to him in the northern part of the crypt, beckoning him to come to him; but he, seized with fearful dread of the living and deceased lord, began to gaze at him with fearful eyes. When questioned by him why he was thus bending his eyes upon him, he replied: "Behold, I see my elder Adalbero prepared for mass, and calling me to him." But he said: "Hasten, fulfill his command." When he came to him, he said: "Rambert, tell your lord the bishop that he will receive a reward from the Lord for the prayers and alms he has faithfully sent to me, and tell him this sign, that Fortunatus and I, with the Lord's permission, will sanctify the chrism with him at the next Lord's Supper, and that the work of this crypt will be brought to ruin; yet, he should not cease to strive to establish it firmly in the future. Also, I admonish the brothers to remember that they pledged to labor for me with diligent and constant prayer, without force, and that if they have not done so, and if they do not amend this, they should know that they will have to give an account of this before the Lord; and you shall sing one psalm for me daily, without caution, and I will admonish you to amend this." Meanwhile, the bishop, occupied with royal duties, directed his course to the court, and there, long detained among the courtiers with worthy honor, finally, having requested a healthy permission, returned home, and found the work whose effect he hoped to see entirely fallen and overturned, according to the aforementioned account of Rambert. Then, indeed, having laid more careful foundations, he firmly completed it.

However, at another time, when in the town of Waringa, having customarily called in the early morning to fulfill the psalmody with the same Rambert, the same brother began to be timidly stirred with downcast eyes. When questioned by him, he replied, saying: "Behold, I see my elder Adalberon in the same way as I saw him before, commanding me to serve him at mass." He immediately rising, having closed the doors, withdrew from the church until this vision came to an end. Moreover, another vision, which we have dedicated to saying happened to many brothers speaking the truth, we ought not to consign to oblivion. For when a religious man diligently strove to perform the ministry of the sacraments on Easter day, with a multitude of clerics arriving, and with a certain Heilricus, a presbyter and cantor, being present, the right hand appeared with the right hand of the bishop sanctifying the sacraments. When the mass was completed, the aforementioned Heilricus fell at his feet in his chamber and explained this vision more carelessly than he should have in the presence of laymen. When he responded, he said: "It would have been more useful for you to have kept silent than to speak;" and amazed by this response, he withdrew from him, and sat down at the table that is located before his chamber, and immediately his eyes began to shed tears with great intensity, and they remained in that outpouring until they were entirely deprived of the present light.

II. At another time, on the night preceding the holy day of the Lord's Supper, as if in a dream he heard a voice speaking to him: "Ulrich, bishop, know that today you will receive guests." And awakened by the voice, he began to consider who those guests might be. While he was sleeping, he heard the words of the speaker: "The Lord's eyes have seen your prayers and your alms, and therefore you have been commended to your two predecessors Fortunatus and Adalberon, so that they may assist you today and henceforth in these sacred solemnities while you celebrate the holy mysteries, and may bless them with you." When morning came, after the other mysteries had been performed as is customary, while consecrating the sacraments with the orders of ministers surrounding him, he and some of the more devout among those present saw the right hand of the Lord consecrating the sacraments with him and imposing the sign of the cross; to whom, because he knew them through the spirit, as they were about to receive the viaticum from him, he placed a finger over his mouth so that they might keep silent about the vision. To these, also, after calling them to himself, he secretly announced what had been said to him in the night, and commanded that, while he lived, neither what was seen nor what was secretly heard should be revealed to anyone, if they wished to continue having this present life.

I do not consider it good to keep silent about the miracles of a greater vision manifested to oneself. Because one night, when he had placed his body on the bed to sleep, he saw Saint Afra in great beauty, dressed in a beautiful tunic and girded, standing before him and saying: "Arise and follow me." And saying this, she led him to a field commonly called Lechfeld. There he found Saint Peter, the prince of the apostles, with a great multitude of bishops and other saints, and those whom he had not seen before but recognized well by the nod of God, holding a synodal discussion with them, arranging great and innumerable matters, and judging the living Duke Arnolph of Bavaria, who was accused legally of the destruction of many monasteries, which he had divided into the benefits of laypeople, and showing him two very noble swords, one with a hilt and the other without, and speaking thus: "Tell King Henry, the sword that is without a hilt signifies a king who will hold the kingdom without pontifical blessing; however, the one with a hilt will hold the reins of the kingdom with divine blessing." When this aforementioned synod was finished, the martyr of God showed him the places of the castles where later Otto, the still reigning king, had royal conversations with the peoples of various provinces; where King Berengar of Lombardy and his son Adalbert presented themselves with many bishops and submitted to his dominion. He also indicated to him the impending incursion of the Hungarians, and the places of battle, and although laboriously, he announced that victory had been granted to the Christians. After this vision was completed, he released him, having been placed back on the bed. He himself, having returned to himself, contemplated, reverently recalling the words of the illustrious seer who was caught up to the secrets of the third heaven saying: Whether in the body or out of the body (2 Cor. XII), etc. This vision, however, was revealed to him by a few wise men and those familiar to him. Later, approaching the king's court, he was subjected to his service as usual, until King Henry finished his present life. Thus, when Otto, his son, was elevated to the kingdom, he endeavored to impart the same diligence of service and firmness of faith to all as he had to his father. At that time, Bishop Ulrich had a nephew named Adalbero, of good character, son of his sister Luitgarde, entrusted to a most learned master, Benedict the monk, for the education in the knowledge of grammar and other books. When he had been taught and educated in all the advancements of good knowledge and discipline to the stature of manhood, he was immediately exempted from school, presented to the emperor by his uncle the bishop, and committed into his hands of mercy, serving the royal office with such diligence and decency until the emperor was pleased with his service in ecclesiastical and secular matters. Because of this certain diligence of his daily service, it was granted to his holy uncle Bishop Ulrich that the aforementioned Adalbero, in his stead, should carry out hostile journeys with the episcopal militia at the will of the emperor, and should remain in the emperor's court in his stead, so that the aforementioned prelate might be allowed to occupy himself with the service of God, the custody of the entrusted flock, and the benefits of the church, and with prayers and almsgiving according to his desire. Indeed, as much as he perceived himself to be more free from secular cares, he endeavored to make himself more obligated to the will of God. The daily course with the matriculories in the choir of that same matricula was carefully observed by him, whenever other occupations allowed him to remain at home. Moreover, he was accustomed to complete one course in honor of Saint Mary, the Mother of God, another about the Holy Cross, a third about all saints, and many other psalms, and to complete the entire psalter every day, unless some unavoidable necessity impeded him. However, he did not cease to sing three or two or one Masses daily, according to the span of time, unless illness of the body or some good study withdrew him.

III. On many occasions, he abstained from meat, yet he generously provided for others who were eating with him. During daily meals, when he sat at the table with his companions, the first servings of bread and food, for the most part, were distributed to the poor by some cleric to whom these were entrusted, except for the lame and the weak who, walking in beds and on stools, received their daily sustenance in his presence from the best foods and drinks. However, no one else who ate in his presence, whether known or unknown, left hungry or thirsty, unless it happened sometimes due to the negligence or stubbornness of the servants against the bishop's will. Guests who came to him were received with joy and such cheerfulness of countenance and spirit, and were cared for in all things, as was best for them, knowing that they had received Christ in them, as He said: I was a stranger, and you welcomed me (Matthew 25). The emperor's vassals, coming from him or returning to him, were received with the utmost honor, and they feasted to such an extent that neither they nor their beasts were burdened by any need, and having received the necessary supplies for their journey, they returned to him joyfully. Monks, clerics, and holy women visiting him were loved by him as sons, and he abundantly refreshed them with spiritual and bodily nourishment, allowing them to stay with him as long as it pleased them, and at an appropriate time he dismissed them all joyfully. He commanded his clerics from his household, whether of humble birth or nobler, to be nurtured and taught with the utmost diligence, and he enriched those among them whom he recognized as worthy of honor with ministries and appropriate benefits. The laypeople subject to his authority always dwelled with him with all honor and joy, fearing no deception from him, but firmly believing and knowing for certain that whatever he had promised them, he had swiftly fulfilled with the Lord's consent. From his entrusted household, anyone who came before him exclaiming that he had been unjustly oppressed or stripped, or wronged in some way by his lord to whom he had been granted a benefit, whether by his servant or by anyone else, he listened to cautiously; and when he learned that an injustice had been done against him, he firmly commanded that the wrong done to him be quickly rectified, and he did not cease until it was accomplished. He firmly allowed the legitimate rights of the entire household, which he had used for his ancestors, to be upheld, and permitted no man of any power dwelling under his authority to take this from him. He never allowed his mind to succumb to idle leisure, unless he devised or accomplished something useful, whether concerning the church, which he found completely dilapidated, or its adornment, or the preparations for altars and clerics, and the discipline of canons and the school, concerning the sustenance and salvation of the household, and how he could fortify the city, which he found surrounded by inept valleys and rotten wood, because in those times the savagery of the Hungarians was raging in these provinces like demons. Although he dealt with all these matters externally in consultation with his faithful, he was, however, inwardly inflamed with the heat of divine love, and he eagerly hastened to associate himself with God through vigils, prayers, fasting, and almsgiving, always placing a woolen garment on his skin and following the rule of the monks. After Compline, he never, at the request of any man, consented to eat or drink, indulging in the pleasure of his body. He did not sleep on the softness of a featherbed, but rested on a mat or on carpets laid beneath him. At night, when the first sign sounded, he rose and completed the aforementioned tasks with great caution.

IV. The time of Lent was celebrated with such devotion that words are not sufficient to describe it; nevertheless, we should not entirely omit what we have seen. After the morning praises were completed, as dawn began to break, he began to chant the psalter with other prayers, and after completing that and the litany, he firmly continued with other prayers until the signal for the vigil of the dead sounded. Upon hearing it, he immediately rose and celebrated the Vigil with the brothers and the First Hour; after the First Hour was completed, while the brothers, as was customary, were carrying the cross, he remained in the church and chanted a shortened book of psalms with other prayers until the brothers returned with the cross and began to celebrate the Mass of sacrifice, he himself devoutly offering the sacrifice to God, humbly kissing the hand of the priest. After the Mass was completed, he fulfilled the Third Hour with the brothers; when the brothers went to the chapter, he remained in the church as was customary until the signal for the Sixth Hour sounded. When the sixth hour was completed, he circled the altars with reverence, singing "Have mercy on me, O God," and "Out of the depths"; then he finally returned to his room to wash his face and prepare for Mass. After the celebrations of the Masses were completed and Vespers were sung, he went to the hospice of the poor, washed the feet of twelve poor men, and gave each of them a denarius from his purse. Returning from there, he sat down to eat, where there was no shortage of reading, nor of the multitude of the aforementioned poor. He joyfully took what was offered and distributed it with great cheer to those who remained with him, recalling the Apostle's words: "For God loves a cheerful giver" (2 Cor. 9). For each one, he provided what he thought they would gladly receive. After the meal was finished, and all who were with him were made joyful, he recited Compline at the appropriate time, and in addition, after completing other prayers, he quietly repeated the secrets of his chamber, avoiding all conversation except with God and His saints until the completion of the First Hour of the next day. In this way, he completed the days of Lent, up to the day of indulgence they call Palm Sunday. On that day, early in the morning, he would come to St. Afra, if he had not stayed there the previous night, he would sing the Mass of the Holy Trinity, and bless the branches of palms and various foliage, and with the Gospel and crosses and banners, and with the image of the Lord sitting on a donkey, he would proceed with the clerics and a multitude of people carrying palm branches in their hands, and with hymns composed in honor of that day, and with great splendor he would go up to the hill known as Perleich, where a choir of canons would come to meet him with great beauty, along with the citizens who had remained in the city, and those who wished to join him from the surrounding towns, there, to imitate the humility of the children and other people, spreading the way with palm branches and their garments. After these things were completed, the holy man made a most fitting admonition about the passion of the Lord to all, to the point that he often wept, and through his weeping, he made many weep. After the admonition was completed, all together praising God arrived at the mother church, where they celebrated Mass with him, and from there all returned to their places. Afterward, during those three consecutive days, he was accustomed to hold a synodal meeting, since the canons prescribe that bishops' councils should be held twice a year: one on the 15th of the Kalends of October, and the other in the fourth week after Easter; he decided to complete this during this time, so that no obstacle would impede its completion in the future, and so that during the Lord's Supper, the same multitude of clerics and people might more fully and honorably sanctify the chrism and oil. On that day, at the third hour, all the clerics, dressed in their most solemn attire, came to the church, and he, gloriously prepared for the service of God, began to devoutly perform the sacred mystery with them, after reading the Gospel, and making an admonition to the people, and receiving the confession of the people, he humbly granted them indulgence, and the entire synod, offering the oblation, carefully fulfilled it according to the order, up to the blessing of the chrism and oil; this he did with great reverence, having it brought to him, with crosses and boys carrying it hidden under a pall, and with candles, with verses beautifully sung for this ministry, and with a procession of twelve priests, who were to persevere in their ministry with him until the end of the Mass. When it was rightly brought to him, he humbly received it, and asked the whole synod that when he blessed the cross over it, they too, along with the same priests who were in the procession and assisting him, would not cease to bless, and he asked the rest of the people to sing the Our Father with great humility. After this blessing, and the people being refreshed with the sacred viaticum, after Vespers were completed, he came to the sacrarium to dispense the chrism and oil to the clerics. After dispensing these, he went to the hospice of the poor and ministered to them as was his custom. Then he walked to the church and came before the sacrarium, where he clothed twelve poor men with new garments brought by the chamberlain, and dispensed a heap of alms to others, and on that day he did not allow anyone to leave empty-handed, although a great multitude was present. Afterward, he came to food, and with all those who remained with him, he began to wash the feet of his disciples, following the example of the Lord. After the washing was completed with appropriate antiphons, verses, and readings, he sufficiently offered the best cups stored in his cellars with great love and humility, and after Compline was completed, he commended his weary limbs in the service of God to the rest of the bed. On the day of preparation, after the hours were carefully completed in order, omitting other courses, as on the day of the Lord's Supper, except for those pertaining to that day, he hastened to complete the psalter early in the morning, and, having performed the sacred mystery of God, and having fed the people with the sacred body of Christ, and, as was customary, having buried what remained, he again completed the psalter by walking among the churches, chanting, and at the evening hour, without a table and table goods, he began to refresh himself in his room with bread and beer, and he commanded that bread and beer be offered to each one who was with him according to their desire. On the most holy Saturday, after the nocturnal offices were completed, and the beloved psalter was read, he entered the prepared bath, which he never used at that time except on the Saturday before Lent and in the middle of Lent, and on that day. After the washing of the body was completed, and having put on prepared garments, he solemnly prepared himself for the sacred office, and determined that the entire clergy should be ready with him at the ninth hour of the day, and immediately, after reading the triple litany, having sanctified the candle and completed the readings and the tract, he went with great honor to the church of St. John the Baptist to consecrate the baptism, having baptized three boys there with the sevenfold litany, he returned to the sacrarium to prepare for Mass, while the clergy were singing in the choir. After the solemnities of the Masses were solemnly completed with Vespers, and the body of Christ was dispensed, and the sacred vestments were laid aside, on that day he sat at the table prepared for refreshment with a great multitude, and after abundantly refreshing all with joy, he allowed them to return to their lodgings. As the most desirable and most holy Easter day approached, after the First Hour, he entered the church of St. Ambrose, where on the day of Preparation he had placed the body of Christ on the stone, and there he celebrated the Mass of the Holy Trinity with a few clerics: after the Mass was completed, he went before the clergy, who were gathered in the supper next to that same church, dressed in the most solemn vestments, carrying with him the body of Christ and the Gospel, and candles, and with the appropriate salutation of verses sung by the boys, he proceeded through the atrium to the church of St. John the Baptist, where he chanted the Third Hour, and from there with antiphons most fittingly composed in honor of this day, he arrived to celebrate Mass with the most beautiful procession, with pairs walking together according to the order. Therefore, after the Mass was devoutly and religiously chanted, with all receiving the sacraments of Christ and returning to their places, he approached the food, where he found three tables prepared with all decorum: one at which he was accustomed to sit with those he could, another for the matrons, and the third for the congregation of holy Afra. Having sanctified the food, he dispensed the lamb's meat and pieces of lard among those blessed during the solemnities of the Mass, and then finally took food with them with all joy. At the appointed time, the musicians came, of such a copious multitude that they nearly filled the hall standing in order, and they completed three modes of music. With these joys multiplied, the canons, at the bishop's prompting, receiving and asking for charity, sang one responsory about the resurrection of the Lord in the meantime. And when this charity was completed, the congregation of St. Afra did likewise at the other table. As evening approached, he commanded that cups be joyfully offered to himself and those sitting with him, and he asked everyone to drink charitably the third cup, and having received it with charity, the entire clergy sang the third responsory together with joy. After this was sung, the canons rose singing a hymn, so that they could suitably prepare to arrive at Vespers. After Vespers were completed, the bishop, with guests and soldiers, returned to his house to cheer them all. In the morning, which is the day of the moon, the entire clergy gathered at St. Afra to honorably receive the coming bishop dressed in the most beautiful attire, for it was his custom to serve God in solemnities of the sacred Mass there on that day, and after the solemnities of the sacred Masses were completed, he would confirm the multitude of people gathered there with the sacred chrism, and after these things were completed, he returned to the city, where he devoutly celebrated the entire Easter week.

V. After the solemnity of Easter was finished, when the necessity of some matter required that he could legitimately proceed to other places or to monasteries pertaining to the episcopate, Wthinuvanc, Staphense, Fauces, Wissintesteiga, Heuvibach (which he never granted as a benefit to laymen, unless he had conceded to someone from this district in which his monastery is situated, from external places pertaining to the same monasteries, so that he could have an advocate for the monastery there, to defend ecclesiastical matters from him, but he retained all the best things under his authority, namely for the reason that he would have the opportunity to visit them and stay there, and to correct what was necessary in the stipends), he was sitting on a throne above a constructed cart, hanging from the shoulders of a wagon in iron, and with him was one cleric from his chaplains, who had sung psalms with him all day long. He did not begin to proceed in this way primarily unless he could still caballicare, but so that he might be separated from the people, lest he be hindered in the singing of their psalms by their foolish conversations. Moreover, he always commanded that some of his wisest presbyters accompany him, and only from the chaplains so that he could perform the service of God decorously every day. Likewise, he always wanted to have some of his wisest vassals with him, in case any business concerning ecclesiastical or secular matters came to be discussed, so that he would always be prepared to handle and govern cautiously with their counsel. There were also always chosen from the household those who would have been the leaders for the oxen pulling, and they would carefully observe him before and behind, to the right and to the left, of whom he daily provided such an abundance of provisions through himself and his ministers in his presence that it could suffice for a triple number of men. The most loving company of the poor also always went with him among his places; they had the virtue of caballicandi and proceeded in very cautious walks. Others, however, continued in the vehicles in which they were accustomed to go, as the episcopal ministries were carried by the carts. He himself carefully arranged the lodgings and all the provisions daily through one of his faithful. Never, however, did he remain idle in any of the aforementioned monasteries, unless he labored in the buildings of the church, or cloisters, or other buildings, or walls that had been previously prepared and with collected furnishings. Moreover, he was entirely devoted to governing and arranging the life of the monks or canons serving God in the same monastery and did not permit the dissolution of the family rights in any way. He also did not neglect to confer the gifts of the Holy Spirit, where there was necessity, with the confirmation of chrism.

VI. However, it was both pleasing and necessary for the peoples, in the fourth year, according to the constitution of the canons, to visit his diocese entrusted to him for the purpose of ruling, preaching, and confirming, in the same manner as we have previously mentioned, he sat on a chair placed on a carpet, and sang psalms in the usual manner, imitating that eunuch who, sitting on his chariot, was reading the prophet Isaiah as he went along the road, to whom Philip was joined by the Holy Spirit's prompting, and who, having been preached to and baptized by him, received the faith of the Holy Trinity, considering for certain how much he had withdrawn from human conversations, so that he could make himself closer to the divine. When he arrived at those places where his councils had been announced, he was received with the Gospel, blessed water, ringing bells, and such honor as the strength of those gathered there could provide. Immediately, after the Mass was celebrated, sitting in council, he ordered the people to be called before him, and commanded the wiser and more truthful to inquire by oath what in that parish was worthy of correction, and the sins committed against the laws of Christianity, so that the actions might be made known to him through truthful reports. And when he heard from them any standard of rectitude exceeding knowledge, without regard to persons, according to the judgment of the clergy, he hastened to draw back to the path of righteousness, as much as he could, with the help of Almighty God, and he diligently sought to prune the ill-growing shoots of vices with the sickle of the Word of God, lest the thickets of evil seedlings should have the license to suffocate the harvest of Christ entrusted to him; and he opposed the most suitable remedies for the diseases of vices, but still according to the Word of God saying: "Reprove, entreat, rebuke with all patience and teaching" (II Tim. IV). However, those things which he found to be difficult and insurmountable for his ministers, he attempted to finish with careful direction in their presence, with the help of all who remained with him. And those which he perceived could be converted to a state of rectitude without the disparagement of others, he firmly committed to their governance to be perfected. He, following the rule of his ministry, sought to impose the confirmation of the sacred anointing on the people gathered for this purpose, by the gift of the Holy Spirit. But if the night, creeping in as usual while these things were still incomplete, came upon him, lest any part of the sheep entrusted to him should be burdened by the deprivation of heavenly gifts, he resolved to begin to complete the work with the lights kindled in the name of the Lord. Meanwhile, when such contention arose from the opponents of justice that, with the day departing, the darkness of night was poured out upon the world, lest the councils ventilated there should remain uncorrected, he commanded that the canonical rules be read with the lights kindled, so that the mouths of the opponents of justice might be closed, and all might be fulfilled in the will of God by just judgments. And when the council was completed or confirmed, he returned to the lodgings, and did not taste the meal for the body until alms were distributed by him to the poor through the cleric to whom that obedience was entrusted. However, when the weak came to him, he commanded that an abundant repast be set before them. On certain days, he planned to hold chapters with the clergy in those places where the archpresbyters thought these things could be most suitably done, and where they considered him to be more free from other worldly councils. Having gathered the clergy before him, he cautiously questioned the archpresbyters and deans, and the best he could find among them, how the daily service of God was fulfilled by them, and how the people subject to them were governed in the study of preaching and teaching; how carefully infants were baptized, the sick visited and anointed, and with what compassion the bodies of the deceased were delivered to burial; how the poor and weak were refreshed from the tithes and offerings of the faithful; how they assisted widows and orphans in all their needs; and how diligently they ministered to Christ in hospices and to strangers; if they had women secretly with them, and thus fell into the crime of suspicion; if they pursued hunts with dogs or hawks, if they entered taverns for the sake of eating or drinking; if they engaged in vile jokes; if they loved drunkenness and excessive feasting; if they served in quarrels, contentions, and rivalries; if they participated in secular weddings; or if any of them had indecent ministries in their custom; if they convened at the appointed places on the Kalends, as was the custom of their predecessors, and there fulfilled the usual prayers, and visited their churches at the appointed times; if they had provided obedience to their masters, and had striven to remain devout and suitable in all their ministry. After the responses were made to the questions, and the truth was perceived, he gratified them standing in the rectitude of the sweetest consolation, and admonished them with gentle discourse not to deviate from the standard of justice; he terrified the erring brothers walking in the wrong paths with worthy corrections, and commanded them to omit the usual vices afterward.

VII. However, among those who had properties in their episcopate, whoever among the religious wished to establish a church for the love of Christ, and had built it with the granted permission from the same holy bishop, he readily gave his consent to each one's petition, provided that the person did not delay in giving a legitimate endowment of lands and possessions to his highness in the presence of the citizens and truthful witnesses, so that the truth of the matter would not be obscured later; also for the reason that the rights of other neighboring churches would not be diminished in any way because of that new church. After the consecration was completed and the endowment was given, he entrusted the management of the altar to the presbyter there, and firmly committed the advocacy of the church to a legitimate heir with a cloth imposed. He did not demand any offering of gifts, unless the presbyter of that church would spontaneously obtain something for his honor and good will.

VIII. At a certain time, Jesus, obeying the precepts, when he had decided to fulfill the office of his ministry in the district of Aldegowe, certain men from that district came to him, lamenting and saying: "Our fathers built a small church from stones, mortar, and wood in their property which they left to us, wishing it to be dedicated to God and His saints, and that they might merit to hear the celebration of sacred offices there, because this place is situated in a great desolation of wilderness. But due to the difficulty of the road and their poverty, they have never been able to bring a bishop to consecrate the aforementioned church." Upon hearing this, the servant of God, with a cheerful countenance, said: "Can you now acquire what is necessary for the consecration of the church?" They, relying on the consolation of their friends, responded: "We can." To which he replied: "Leaving me as the guide of the way, go ahead, and I will come to assist your necessity there, and, with God's help, I will consecrate the church." The next day, after the consecration was completed, the citizens themselves came before him, offering gifts according to their means; seeing these, he smiled and said: "I have come here not for the love of any gift, but to attend to your necessity and that the service of God may be multiplied in this place. Keep these offered for your benefit, and as you grow in the service of God, remain in peace." Saying this, he withdrew and made no complaint about the difficulty of the road, except as if rejoicing.

IX. Truly, he, insisting on the studies of good works, spiritually refreshed all who dwelt with him with the most benevolent exhortation, teaching that not only in words but also in deeds each one should love the Lord perfectly with all their strength, and prefer nothing to His love, and honor their neighbor as themselves, and their father and mother; moreover, he urged all men of good will, of whom the angelic multitude sings, saying: "And on earth peace to men of good will" (Luke II); but he would resist the wicked in all their evil deeds, according to the holy prophet David, who says: "The wicked is brought to nothing in his presence; but He glorifies those who fear the Lord" (Psalm XIV); that what one would not want for oneself, one should not do to another; that he should frequently visit the churches of God with devotion of mind and humility and with offerings, and there strive to cry out to God with the effusion of tears for the remission of his sins and for all his just needs. Furthermore, he advised to seek forgiveness from enemies, according to the Lord's Prayer, saying: "Forgive us our debts, as we also have forgiven our debtors" (Matthew VI); and according to the Gospel: "So will my heavenly Father do to you, if each of you does not forgive his brother from his heart" (Matthew XVIII); and again: "Forgive, and you will be forgiven" (Luke VI). He hastened to present the tithes of all his labors to the Lord and His saints, and to the churches to which they were assigned, lest they fall into the guilt of Cain the fratricide with great caution. He also advised to venerate Sundays and other solemnities of the year not only in abstaining from servile works but also from all vices, with the utmost devotion; to receive the Eucharist continually, and to present oneself purified before receiving; and to strive to keep oneself pure after reception. He admonished that the days of Lent and other fasts established of old, and newly found with consensus, should be observed with all devotion by all, to make self-denial and to follow the footsteps of Christ, to chastise the body, to not love delights, to refresh the hungry and thirsty with food and drink, to provide clothing for the naked, to visit the sick and those in distress, to grant shelter to the needy and the wandering, and to provide what is necessary out of love for Christ, to visit orphans and widows in their tribulations, and to assist them in all their needs, to not retain malice in the heart, and to not provoke anyone to anger with words, to lay aside anger, to leave vengeance to the Lord, to not repay evil for evil, nor to exacerbate any injury, to not speak ill of those who speak ill of them, but rather to bless, and to endure persecution for righteousness, to recall those who are in discord and enmity to the concord of unanimity, to resist those who resist God, and to provide aid to those who fight with faith, so that none may be ensnared by the eight principal vices which infest all kinds of men. Moreover, when asked what the eight principal vices were, he replied not only to them but also to those who still remained in hesitation, stating the eight vices, saying: The first is gluttony, that is, the gluttony of the belly, with its offspring: feasting and drunkenness; the second is fornication, with its offspring: foul speech, scurrility, and foolishness; the third is avarice, that is, love of money, with its offspring: lying, fraud, theft, perjury, the desire for filthy gain, false testimony, violence, inhumanity, voracity, and rapacity; the fourth is anger, with its offspring: homicide, shouting, and indignation; the fifth is sadness, with its offspring: rancor, cowardice, bitterness, and despair; the sixth is acedia, with its offspring: idleness, sleepiness, importunity, restlessness, wandering, instability of mind and body, verbosity, and curiosity; the seventh is vainglory, with its offspring: contention, heresy, boasting, and presumption of novelties; the eighth is pride, with its offspring: contempt, envy, disobedience, blasphemy, murmuring, backbiting, and enmity. He said that blessed is he who does not stumble in these snares of vices. Moreover, he advised to carefully perceive and firmly implant in the innermost thoughts the eight most well-known beatitudes enumerated by God in the Gospel, so that in times of temptation the power may not be granted to the wicked spirits to uproot them, but that each one may be raised up by the consolations of their heavenly desires; and to always give praises and thanks to the Lamb of Almighty God, Christ, who takes away the sins of the world, day and night with many desires and all their strength, because He is worthy, by His incarnation, nativity, baptism, crucifixion, burial, resurrection, and ascension, to loose the seals of the seven sealed books, shown in vision to the holy apostle John on the island of Patmos. Moreover, he earnestly and humbly requested the goodwill of all in common: if there were any who felt they had grown a harvest of some virtues within themselves, they should apply themselves not to their own merits, but to the mercy of Almighty God, lest they be suddenly destroyed by the hail of pride, but rather, with timely maturity, be placed in the barns of Christ, protected by the Holy Spirit. He advised to guard the mouth from evil or corrupt speech, to gladly listen to holy readings, to confess their past sins to God daily with groaning and tears, and to amend themselves henceforth, to not fulfill the desires of the flesh, to break their own will, to obey the commands of priests, even if they, God forbid! act otherwise, imitating those of whom the Lord says: "For they say, and do not do" (Matthew XXIII). He urged to love chastity, to hate no one, to not have envy and jealousy, to not cultivate quarrels, to hate pride, to revere the elders, to love the younger, to have the fear of the Lord in the heart and soul without interruption, to believe that the eyes of the Lord see all, and His ears hear all, as the Psalmist says: "Behold, the eyes of the Lord are upon the righteous, and His ears are open to their prayers; but the face of the Lord is against those who do evil, to cut off the remembrance of them from the earth" (Psalm XXXIII). He always kept before his eyes the day of his death and the day of the final judgment, in which the Lord will say to those who hasten to refresh, clothe, and visit Him in His poor: "Come, you blessed of my Father" (Matthew XXV), etc., but to those negligent in these things, and who do not minister to God in His members: "Depart from me, you cursed, into the eternal fire prepared for the devil and his angels" (Ibid.), always keeping before his eyes the suspect and timid. He often contemplated the punishments prepared for the cursed; and the most wretched place that is always without refreshment, and without brightness, and without sweetness, and will be without end, where their worm does not die, and the fire is not extinguished, where weeping and gnashing of teeth is always heard without interruption, where the devouring flame will always be renewed by the machinations of the devil, where there is absolutely no hope of consolation, but from hour to hour sadness increases, because they cannot find an end to their stay, but they will persevere in anguish without end with those whom they served in this world. However, concerning the blessed of God and those placed at His right hand, how great joys and delights remain, one should always think, as much as is possible for human minds, of which it is written: "What no eye has seen, nor ear heard, nor the heart of man ascended, what God has prepared for those who love Him" (I Cor. II). Where the choirs of angelic hymns will shine with ineffable brightness; where the height of the patriarchs will rejoice in worthy honor; where the true order of the prophets, having fulfilled their prophecies in full, does not cease to give thanks to God; where the judge of the chorus of apostles, having received the promised reward beforehand, will rejoice forever; where the martyrs, crowned with the palm of martyrdom, enjoy eternal consolation; where the confessors, with their rewards multiplied, persist in praises of God; where the virgins bear a hundredfold fruit in reward, and widows are honored with sixtyfold fruit in restitution; where monks, having renounced all worldly things, with the hungry and thirsty seeking the justice of God, having fulfilled their desires, will not cease to insist on the praises of God; where the penitents, having laid aside the burdens of their sins, will rejoice without end praising God; where children following the Lamb in white, harmonizing with the angels under the throne, do not cease to sing praises to God; where the most glorious virgin, the Mother of God, Mary, exalted above the choirs of angels, is seen cheering all with inestimable brightness and beauty; where the righteous will shine like the sun, and all the saints will see their Creator and all creatures, rejoicing face to face in His brightness, taking away all fear and all sorrow and sadness, and all adversity. In that kingdom, the light of the sun, moon, and stars will not be necessary; hunger and thirst will harm no one, nor will cold or heat weary anyone, nor will sickness and pain come to anyone, nor will the misery of impending old age be feared, but just as at the day of judgment the bodies of the dead will rise in the measure of the fullness of Christ's age, they will also remain in that impassibility and beauty. Weddings will not be celebrated there, and the progeny of men will not multiply afterwards, but the complete number of the just will not diminish, but will be kept in joy without end; they will no longer fear the snares of the devil, nor will they need forgiveness of sins any longer; just as the angels will remain in the impassibility of their original condition, so will men, after the resurrection, equal to the angels, persevere in sobriety and immutability in the city of our God, built on His holy mountain, which is said to be adorned and founded with twelve precious stones, the names and order of which the holy apostle and evangelist John enumerates in the Apocalypse: where he says that the first foundation is jasper, which is said to drive away all phantoms, in which the greenness of faith is designated; the second is sapphire, which designates the hope of heavenly bliss; the third is chalcedony, which figures the flame of inner charity; in the fourth, emerald, which figures the strong confession of the same faith amid adversities; in the fifth, sardonyx, signifying humility among the virtues of the saints; in the sixth, sardius, in which the blood of the holy martyrs is expressed; in the seventh, chrysolite, in which the spiritual preaching among miracles is figured; in the eighth, beryl, in which the perfect work of the preachers is signified; in the ninth, topaz, in which their burning contemplation is shown; in the tenth, chrysoprase, which signifies both the work and reward of the blessed martyrs; in the eleventh, hyacinth, which figures the heavenly elevation to the heights, and the descent to the humble; in the twelfth, amethyst, which designates the memory of the heavenly kingdom in the mind of the humble. This position of the twelve stones signifies the firmness of the apostles, who are placed as the foundation of the Church, as the Savior of the world said to the blessed Peter: "You are Peter, and upon this rock I will build my Church" (Matthew XVI). By saying this to Peter, He made it known to all the apostles that His Church was to be built upon them, whose sound has gone out into all the earth, and their words to the ends of the world. If the apostles are the foundation of the house of God, and all of Christianity is the building of that temple, it must remain, as the Apostle says: "The temple of God is holy, which you are, and you are the building of God" (I Cor. III), let us all strive with all our strength to join ourselves to the Builder and Dweller, so that, with our teachers placed on the foundation, by His grace, we may be worthy to be built upon; that among the elect stones placed, and joined to the aforementioned orders, we may be seen; that we may be worthy to praise our Creator and Redeemer, the judge of the living and the dead, seeing Him face to face, through infinite ages of ages. Amen.

X. As his reputation for goodness spread far and wide, and the devil saw him standing at this pinnacle of virtues, he strove with all kinds of malice to plunge him into some abyss of difficulty and hinder him from his good endeavors. At that time, Liutolf, the son of Otto, the glorious king, was the duke of the Alamanni, whose father had previously subjected all the peoples of the regions under his dominion to an oath before the end of his life; the uncle of Liutolf, Heinrich, the king's brother, was the duke of the Noricans. However, due to the boundaries of their regions, they began to engage in quarrels and disputes at the suggestion of wicked men. When the king could not in any way bring them back to concord and peace, he turned to his son for help and assistance against his brother. However, when his son, along with all those he could gather, was striving to resist him and was attempting to act as an exile from royal power, Heinrich, the aforementioned duke, entrusted the city of Regensburg and the entire region of Noricum to Count Arnulf of the Palatinate and his other loyal subjects, and went to the king. While he was delaying there, the aforementioned Arnulf, with a multitude of people, deceitfully took Regensburg along with the other cities and with the crowd of people, and subjected them all under the power of Liutolf. When the king learned of this, he invaded Bavaria hostilely with his brother Heinrich to restore him to the honor of his previous power. The aforementioned prelate, Ulrich, whose firm loyalty had never been separated from the aid of the king, upon learning this, left part of his vassals in the city of Augsburg, and having arranged other matters, with whom he could, disregarding his vehicle, rode to the service of the king, and came sagaciously into the region of Noricum, without being able to have a suitable opportunity to return. Meanwhile, Arnulf, having gathered a multitude, went to Augsburg and plundered all the goods he could take with him, and brought back some of the soldiers of the bishop who had been captured to Bavaria. However, when the king returned from the region of Bavaria, and the bishop wanted to return to his own, he did not consider that he could defend himself in the city of Augsburg with a small multitude, because almost the entire episcopate was being divided as a benefit to foreigners by Liutolf and his followers; some of the bishop's soldiers were captured, some were separated from him by wicked persuasion, and some were reduced to poverty by plundering, so that they could not assist him according to their will. Those who remained with him, strengthened by their discussions, devised a healthy plan to leave the city of Augsburg, to build a castle called Menichingen, and to strive to defend themselves there against their adversaries. Then indeed, he remained enclosed in the city of Augsburg for only one night; the next day he immediately went to the aforementioned castle, which was entirely deserted both inside and outside without buildings. Although certainly the winter had been harsh, nevertheless in that place, hastily set up in tents and huts, they waited until the gathered household surrounded the castle with wood and constructed suitable buildings inside according to their possibilities. Therefore, Arnulf and all who were with him, opposing the royal power from all sides, upon learning this, sent envoys, if he wanted to have safety for himself and his own, he would not delay to submit himself to the power of Liutolf without doubt, and that he would abandon the construction of the aforementioned castle with his men; because at that time in the entire region of the Swabians, no one remained in aid of the king, except Count Adalpert, with those subject to him, and Theodpald, the brother of the religious bishop, and therefore they thought that by their decree he could not acquire any virtue of resistance. He, using wise counsel with his own, mitigated their anger and sieges altogether with various promises and very humble responses, and sometimes giving hostages and receiving them back again to himself, until, having built the castle and renewed the fortifications, he estimated that he could defend himself against their fury with his own in the fortification of that place. When, however, the negotiations for a response could no longer be prolonged, then he clearly confessed that, as he had begun, he wished to endure in the will of the king. Then the aforementioned Arnulf, the son of Duke Arnulf, having gathered the multitude of those unfortunate ones who had previously plundered the city of Augsburg, and others in whose help he then trusted, sought to force the venerable bishop, besieged in the castle, to submit to Liutolf. Upon learning this, the bishop, on the contrary, sent envoys, promising much money, demanding that upon their return they might be allowed to remain in peace; otherwise, if they refused peace, he commanded those same envoys to bind his parishioners by the ban of Christianity, so that they should not presume to invade the places of Saint Mary, situated in his episcopate. However, those who were denied money and postponed the ban of Christianity did not wish to abandon their ill-begun endeavor, but on the Sunday when it is customary for clerics to eat meat before Lent, and from then until the holy time of Easter to avoid it, they hostilely invaded the estate of Saint Mary and besieged the bishop. However, he, remaining diligently in the service of God day and night, casting off fear and trusting in God, considering their besiegements as nothing, firmly persevered in the predestined plan. This siege, when it became known to Count Adalpert and Theodpald, the brother of the bishop, gathered a phalanx of people, and on the first day of Lent, which is a Monday, they attacked the enemy camp at dawn. But those who had not thought that this could happen before were found unprepared for battle, and, struck by sudden fear, they sought to escape, leaving behind their spoils. However, those following them captured Hermann, the brother of Arnulf, killed some in the camp, and others they killed as they pursued them further. With the majority of them slain, and the others fleeing, none of them had confidence to defend themselves, except one named Egilolf; in fleeing, he inflicted a slight wound on the arm of Count Adalpert, from which he also died; his assailant was immediately killed by Liutpert, a vassal of the same Adalpert. Very few of them, bruised by blows and wounded in various ways, nevertheless escaped the danger of death, being carried off by their horses; some of them, miserably constrained by the cold, returned naked in desperation to their own little dwellings. The body of Adalpert, killed by the will of God, was taken by the reverend bishop to the city of Augsburg, and, honoring his soul to God, he buried him in the church of Saint Mary. However, none of those who had previously plundered the city of Augsburg in opposition to the holy Mother of God, Mary, escaped unpunished, except those who did not hesitate to redeem themselves with their own belongings with the indulgence of the reverend bishop.

XI. One of them, tearing his own hands, exhaled his spirit in truth, speaking to his neighbors. Another, having taken a book from the city of Augusta, acquired a pleasing horse for himself and brought it home, showing it to his wife and saying, "I prefer to have this beautiful horse rather than leave the book with which I acquired this in Augusta." To whose words his wife replied, saying, "It would have been useful for you if your hand had not unjustly touched this book." Meanwhile, he was stroking the horse with his hand on its hindquarters, and he was immediately struck by it and died. With these new and unexpected calamities, and many other fearful things having been discovered among the accused by the multitude of people, a great fear seized those who recognized themselves as guilty of the aforementioned plunder of the city of Augusta, not only those who had come there but also those who had received anything unjustly acquired from them. Therefore, turned to repentance and lamentation, they sought to make worthy amends and restitution of the stolen things, and with the urging of the bishop's indulgence, they endeavored to reconcile themselves with Christ and with his holy mother Mary. Not long after, the aforementioned Arnolfus, who presumed to hostilely invade the things of Saint Mary and remained uncorrectable without repentance, went out prepared for battle from the besieged city of Regensburg and was immediately killed at the height of the tumult. Also, a certain man from the bishopric called Eihstetten carried away a part of a very cheap table to his own property, and immediately possessed by a demon, he could find no place to hide from it, neither in the church nor outside the church, nor even sprinkled with holy water, without it always seeming to remain beside him, until, returning to Augusta, he unjustly brought back what he had taken and asked the bishop to impose scourges upon him for the name of Christ, and in addition to grant indulgence for the aforementioned offense, and thus freed from the demon, he departed saved.

XII. I do not wish to withdraw from the initiated taxation, and I would like to retract my pen from the enumeration of both besieged cities and raging wars from all sides, and from the various disturbances, but rather I would like to recount how the Almighty Lord deemed it worthy to liberate His people through the merits of His servants; lest they be led to destruction by the machinations of the devil. When King Otto was in Alamannia, because of those who wanted to oppose his royal authority with Liutolf, his son, he was encamped near a river called Hilara, in the field of a town called Tussa. There, the aforementioned son Liutolf, with another army, came to fight against him, and when they were so close that there remained no hope of ambiguity for either side unless war was engaged, then the beloved of God, Bishop Ulrichus, fully trusting in God, took the religious Bishop Hartbert of the Curiencis Church and began to make peace negotiations between them, pleading for concord of peace, and that the people entrusted to them by God for governance should not be led to destruction for their offenses. With God granting, the minds of both, namely that of father Otto and son Liutolf, turned to softness through the beneficial admonition and teaching of the venerable bishops, and they agreed upon a pact of peace between them; and, with the storm of war mitigated, they returned to their peace. However, having overcome such mentioned burdens of tumult, they thought they could rest for some time in peace. In the very next year, which is the year of the incarnation of our Lord Jesus Christ 965, such a multitude of Hungarians erupted that no one living at that time claimed to have seen such in any region before, and they simultaneously devastated the region of Noricum from the Danube River to the Black Forest, which pertains to the mountains, and when they crossed the Licum and occupied Alamannia, they burned the church of Saint Afra, and plundered the entire province from the Danube to the forest, and set fire to the greatest part up to the Hilara River. They besieged the city of Augusta, which at that time was surrounded by low walls without towers and was not firm in itself. The holy bishop had a very great multitude of the best soldiers gathered within the walls of the city; from their agility and boldness, the city stood firmly, with God's help; when they saw the army of Hungarians surrounding the city to assault it, they wished to go out to meet them, but this the bishop did not consent to, commanding that the gate where the greatest entrance remained firmly be closed. However, the eastern gate, from where one goes to the water, was so occupied by the density of the Hungarians in battle that they thought they could immediately enter: for the soldiers of the bishop, fighting bravely before the gate, resisted them, until one of the Hungarians who was leading the others fell in battle, and, from whose leadership and advance they had great confidence in fighting at that hour, was killed; finally, when the others saw him fall dead to the ground, they, with a great shout and lamentation, took him and returned to their camp. At the hour of battle, the bishop, sitting on his horse, clothed in a stole, unarmed by shield or armor or helmet, stood unscathed and untouched, while darts and stones were flying around him. When the battle was finished, he went around the city and commanded that the houses of war be suitably placed around the city, and that throughout the night they be built, and that the ramparts be renewed as much as time allowed. He, however, spent the entire night in prayer, urging the religious women gathered in the city, that one part of them, with crosses, might devoutly cry out to the Lord within the walls, and the other part, prostrated on the ground, might fervently implore the mercy of the holy Mother of God Mary for the defense of the people and for the liberation of the city. He, however, indulged in a brief rest of sleep for a small part of the night before the hour of Matins, so that, with the morning and Lauds completed, he might be able to offer the sacrificial host to God at the first light of dawn. After the sacred ministry was completed, he refreshed all with the holy viaticum, and humbly urged them to persist in the right faith, not doubting to place their hope in the Lord, indicating to them the various promises of consolation, and announcing the words of the psalmist David, saying: "Even though I walk through the valley of the shadow of death, I will fear no evil, for you are with me" (Psalm 22). After the salutary admonition of the bishop was completed, when the rays of the shining sun first illuminated the breadth of the earth, the army of Hungarians encircled the city to assault it with an indescribable multitude from all sides, bringing various instruments for the demolition of the walls. When they were ready for battle on all sides, and all the defenses of the city were filled with those resisting, some of the Hungarians, threatening others with whips, compelled them to fight, and those, seeing such a multitude in the defenses resisting them, did not dare to join themselves to the walls, so terrified were they. Meanwhile, when they were prepared for battle both inside and outside, Berchtolf, son of Arnolf, came from the castle called Risinesburch to the king of the Hungarians, announcing to him the arrival of the glorious King Otto. When he heard this, he commanded his trumpet to sound throughout the entire army, at whose sound the whole army ceased the battle for the city and hastened to join their king in conversation. When they had made a truce, with God's grace, they ceased from the battle for the city and began to go to meet the glorious king; in such a way that, having overcome him and his, he might return victorious and possess the city and the entire kingdom freely. As King Otto was coming, Count Dietpald, the brother of the bishop, came out at night to meet him with the others who were in the city. Therefore, when the king saw such a great army of Hungarians, he thought that it could not be overcome by men unless Almighty God deemed to kill them, trusting in whose assistance, and strengthened by the consolation of the princes, he began to engage in battle with them, and when both sides fell with mutual slaughter, and those killed who were predestined for destruction by God, glorious victory was given to King Otto by God, for whom nothing is impossible; so that the army of Hungarians turned to flight, losing the strength to fight any longer, and although an incredible number of them had been killed, yet such a multitude of their army remained that those who saw them coming from the ramparts of the city of Augusta thought that they were not being challenged to battle but were returning, until they recognized that they were hastening to return to the further shores of the river Licus. However, the king, following them with his men, killing those he could join himself with, reached Augusta in the evening of the day, and there, leading that night with the bishop, made a great revelation of consolation to him regarding Dietbald, his brother, who had been killed in battle, and regarding others of his relatives killed there. He honored Rihgwin, the son of Dietpald, with the titles of his father, and with the faithful assistance of the bishop, he restored a worthy reward wherever he recognized his desire. In the morning, following the fleeing barbarian bands, he revisited the region of Bavaria, and sending hasty messengers, he commanded to observe all routes and fords of the rivers for their destruction, which was indeed done. They, however, coming there by night, some of them were drowned by those who were in the ships, some were killed, and those who reached the shore were killed by those who were watching the shores, with no way for them to escape, and no deviation could be found that the vengeance of the Lord did not manifestly remain upon them in every place; so that not many days later their kings and princes were captured and taken to Regensburg, in disgrace of their nation, and with many others of their fellow countrymen were hanged on the rack.

XIII. King Otto, holding power in God, confirmed his brother Henry in the kingdom with a powerful hand, and he himself, victorious, was returning to Saxony as was his custom. However, the venerable bishop Ulrich, when the king was departing from Augusta, went to the places where the battle had been fought, seeking his aforementioned brother Dietbald and the noble Reginbold, son of his sister, and finding them, he led them to Augusta, and in the church of Saint Mary before the altar of the virgin Saint Walpurga, he faithfully buried both of them in one grave. After these matters were accomplished as previously stated, the bishop, although he had been wearied by many adversities, took on the effect of good consolation, as is fitting for anyone hoping in God, and began to discuss with his companions how they might most suitably overcome the imminent losses. First, he considered how to support the plundered congregation of clerics in order to fulfill the daily ministry of God's service in the church, for he knew that they had no food, and therefore, with what he himself had been able to obtain through plunder, and what had been sent and offered to him by well-disposed people, he continually provided for them to eat and drink according to his means, and he established various forms of assistance until they themselves mitigated the misery of plunder and brought support to their places through repeated labor. However, their own places, burned by fire and reduced to desolation with crops consumed, he commanded to be renewed through diligent work in the fields and buildings, and the strength of the family complied with his command, thus beginning, and at an appropriate time of usefulness, restored as much as the possibility allowed. The church of Saint Afra, which had been burned by pagans, had still not been rebuilt, but a hut covered with glosses defended the altar from rain and tempests; the tomb of Bishop Simpert, located in the choir next to the steps, remained without a roof: of which covering, warned in a vision, he covered it with wood joined in the manner of a lid. Not long after, he was again admonished not to delay in rebuilding the house of Saint Afra. As he often discussed how it could be most suitably done, and how it could most appropriately adorn the eastern side of the church under the placement of the crypt, no effect of certainty had crept into his mind; with continuous prayers and fasts with domestic and religious priests, he began to devoutly beseech God's mercy in secret that he might be shown the place where the body of Saint Afra had been placed, and whether it would be fitting to compose the crypt in that place where his will was pleased. That his prayer and fast might surely reach the ears of the Lord, according to the song of the holy prophet David: "Behold, the eyes of the Lord are upon the righteous, and his ears are open to their prayers" (Psalm 33), one night in a vision, Saint Afra appeared to him and showed him the place of the placement of her body, as it is written in her passion, from the city of Augusta at the second milestone in the church. However, she forbade the crypt to be made in the predetermined place, because of the relics of the saints, which in that place must await the day of judgment in rest. Informed by this revelation what he should do, he hastily had the walls, mostly laid low by fire, rebuilt, and he added one cubit to the previous height, and adorned the western part of the church with a suitable crypt, commanding that it be carefully measured in his presence, and he did not delay until he had completely covered it with tiles, and adorned the interior of the church with ceilings, and decorated it with bright paintings, and had the ornaments of the church, which had been carried off to the city because of the barbarians and preserved in the mother church, restored.

XIV. That place in the eastern part of the church, which is held in great reverence by God, always remains manifest with certain signs; it seems appropriate to me to connect it here. A certain gardener named Adelpold, while walking among the grass, found a cave, into which, upon entering, he saw a beautiful little building walled up underground, and coming forth, he announced to the bishop, saying: "In this place I can store my vegetables and other necessities." To which he responded by warning, saying: "If you do this, it is not doubtful that you will lose the sense and health of your limbs." However, the gardener, not believing the bishop's words, began to gather the aforementioned things into the same cave without his permission; in doing this, he lost his sense of hearing and sight. When this had been reported to the bishop, he ordered the gardener to be brought to him and said: "Why did you want to occupy that holy place, despising my command?" To which he, although he lacked sense, replied: "I do not deny it; for I know that because of that fault, in which I did not obey your commands, I have incurred this tribulation." The bishop, being compassionate towards his tribulations, granted him forgiveness with a blessing and, by God's grace, restored him to health. Wonderful to say! That gardener was thereafter unable to find that cave in any way. Later, however, the bishop, having summoned the pallbearers, ordered a tomb to be dug for himself on the southern side of the outer wall of the church and to be enclosed with an outer wall, and commanded that an arched wall be constructed above by breaking through the wall of the church, and that a suitable coffin be prepared to cover the body in the tomb, and moreover, that a dense flooring, imperishable for a long time, be carefully joined and placed above. After these preparations for his burial were completed, he was accustomed to visit that place every Friday and to offer sacrifices there, unless some other occupation or absence hindered him. Meanwhile, by God's gracious gift, these regions were illuminated by the concord of peace, and the crowd of persecutions did not prevent benevolent minds from serving God; therefore, he decided to go to Rome, and he arrived there safely, humbly visiting the thresholds of the blessed apostles Peter and Paul with devotion, and there, with abundant prayers and the largesse of alms dispensed to the poor, he was honorably received by Prince Alberic of the Romans, and he stayed there for several days, enriched by frequent ministry and offerings. And when he indicated that he wished to acquire the relics of the saints while staying there, a certain cleric came to him and led him in the silence of the night to where the head of Saint Abundius the martyr was preserved, enclosed in a certain altar of a church, showing him the passion of that saint and presenting the head, he confirmed the sacrament over the relics that the bishop had brought with him, asserting that it was the head of Abundius, whose passion had been read in his presence. When the bishop heard that the sacrament had been completed, he gave the cleric a pleasing reward, and taking the head of Saint Abundius, he brought it back with him to Augusta, where he gloriously enclosed it for the consolation of many. Moreover, he frequently visited the Monastery of Saint Gall, where he had been educated in the sciences of letters, and there he made a feast for the monks serving God, and thence he went to the cell of Saint Meginard to see the holy servant of God, Eberhard, and to assist him and the monks subject to him with whatever needs he could learn of their will. But at the last time, while Eberhard was still alive, when he had to depart from there, having fulfilled the varied expressions of affection, and having received permission with prayers in the church, he went out to the vehicle of his transport; and when he was ready to proceed, and he did not think he would see holy Eberhard any more that day, suddenly, as if hastening, Eberhard came after him, and repeating kisses of charity, with tearful eyes he said: "From this hour you will see me no more, until we are made worthy to see each other in the presence of God, freed from our bodies." Responding to his words, the bishop said: "Sweetest Father, do you now know that I am certainly soon to depart from this world?" To which he replied: "The end of your life does not yet threaten you, but do not doubt that the words I have now spoken to you are true." Having completed these words, the bishop returned, and before he revisited the same cell, Eberhard happily departed from this world.

XV. He also visited the region of the Burgundians at another time, and went to the place of the Agaunenses where Saint Mauritius suffered martyrdom with his followers for the name of the Lord, driven by a great desire for humility. He had previously received a promise from the king of the Burgundians, that he would merit to bring back one of the holy martyrs from his gift and assistance to Augusta. And when he arrived there on Saturday, he found the monastery recently burned by the Saracens, and saw no inhabitants there, except for one burned caretaker of the monastery. As he remained there during the sacred night in praise of God, and in the morning when the rays of the sun first spread light over the earth, he celebrated Mass in honor of the Holy Trinity; when this was completed, he began to celebrate another Mass immediately that was fitting for the veneration of the Lord, and twelve clerics with a multitude of people, having arrived, stood by to hear the celebration of his ministry. When this was done, the holy bishop greeted the same brothers and honored them with gifts, and made known the reason for his coming there. They, perceiving the sweetness of his joy and the piety of his holiness, did not want him to depart deprived of the delightful desire, and they joyfully endowed an open place of the saints' relics in a hollowed rock. When, however, he was returning with the desired permission of the clerics and the most loving farewell of the people, he visited the city of Constantius for the sake of prayer, and from there came to the island of Augia, where he was charitably received by Abbot Aleuvicus and was well provided for in every way. And while they were conversing with each other in friendly dialogue, he made known to him all that had happened to him on his journey. However, the kindness of the abbot, hearing that he was going out for the love of the holy relics, satisfied his desire, not giving him a small part of the body of Saint Mauritius and relics of many other saints, and allowed him to depart joyfully. When he was approaching the city of Augusta, he sent ahead messengers to command that the clerics and the people honorably come to meet the desired gift of the holy relics that he had brought with him, with crosses and incense and blessed water, and that they would gloriously and honorably lead him into the church consecrated in honor of the holy Mother of God, Mary, with praises and fitting melodies. When he was brought there, he was carefully placed by the bishop in a chest covered with gold and silver, for the praise of Almighty God, and for the help of the coming people, in the name of our Lord Jesus Christ, to whom is honor and glory through infinite ages of ages. Amen.

XVI. Serving always in the will of God with such and similar studies, he contended how he could exalt the episcopate he had taken on to govern with all kinds of honors, and tirelessly labored to amplify the service of God and of the holy Mother of God, and therefore everywhere he was preceded by the grace of God, as it is written in the Psalms: "He will fulfill the desire of those who fear him, and he will hear their cry and save them" (Psalm 144); and according to the Apostle saying: "We know that in all things God works for the good of those who love him" (Romans 8). For being honored by the manifold magnificence of God, and strengthened by firm faith, perceiving the desires of his will, he was beneficial in many of their needs, and humbly concealed the power of his capability as much as he could, because many who were afflicted by a mortal disease were restored to health upon receiving the blessing of his holiness, if they did not reveal for what reason they sought the blessing; but those who clearly announced their affliction of necessity, he allowed to depart without the blessing, for the sake of humility, saying: "I am not worthy to free you from this illness."

The oil that was consecrated on the day of the Lord's Supper became so healthful that many who were afflicted with illness, having been anointed with it, were quickly restored to health, and many who had darkness in their eyes and thought themselves deprived of the gift of light in this world, merited to regain the clarity of their sight through the touch of this oil. I discovered these things, without anyone telling me, but I beheld them with my own eyes in many instances. However, it is necessary to mention the recovery of the bishop, for at one time, when he had decided to return from the monastery of Saint Gall to the city of Augsburg, he came to Campidona and was detained by such a severe illness that he could not walk without the assistance of others, and he lacked the strength to take food for the refreshment of his body. Having quickly sent messengers to the city of Augsburg, he commanded that the oil consecrated by him be brought back to him. And when, on the vigil of Pentecost, the messengers returned at the ninth hour of the day, after the congregation of monks had attended the solemn mass, and he himself had heard the sacred mystery within his chamber, the oil was presented to him. After the sacred mystery was completed, the monks were introduced to him in the presence of the clerics who had come there with him, and after singing seven psalms for his illness and devoutly completing the litany, they sent a certain holy monk named Hiltine back to the cloister to anoint him with the holy oil, along with two of his priests. After the anointing was completed, according to the teaching of James the Apostle: "Is anyone among you sick? Let him call for the elders of the church, etc." (James V), the bishop said to the prelate: "With these my anointers and my other companions, serve appropriately in my stead, with the good things that God has granted us today." And when they had taken their places at the table, and the meal had not yet been completed, a messenger came regarding the bishop, saying: "Be of good cheer and rejoice with joy, for our lord the bishop, although he could not take even a morsel of bread for refreshment last week, now, by God's grace, is recovering and has been restored to health." Upon hearing this delightful message, they all together praised God and gave thanks to God, becoming cheerful. When evening came and the evening signal sounded, he immediately rose and walked to the church, where he remained tirelessly in praise of God until the Vespers were completed by the brothers according to the monastic order, and afterwards, strengthened day by day, he was quickly restored to his former health. O how great is the multitude of God's sweetness, who granted him this remedy so swiftly, which he prepared for others for healing and for the forgiveness of sins, so that with his perfect faith the faith of many others might be confirmed!

XVII. I must also convey to you another account in this place, which I learned from Herewig, his chaplain. One day, when he had to cross the river Vindicus for some purpose of utility, and he had been raised above the flood, and all the companions of the bishop were avoiding the crossing and seeking other more suitable fords, the aforementioned Herewig remained alone with him. He crossed the ford that the others had neglected without hesitation, dressed in shoes made of cloth because it was cold, as it was winter. The aforementioned Herewig, having crossed the river, became wet from the waist down, although he was sitting on a horse that was higher than the bishop's, and looking at the bishop's garments to see if they were soaked, he saw not even a single hair in his shoes wet. And he said to the bishop: "I am drenched, and not a hair in your shoes is wet." To which the bishop replied: "Do not presume to tell anyone what you have seen while I am alive." Another time, when he had decided to sail down the Danube to the city of Regensburg for a meeting with Emperor Otto, one day, while the sailors were carelessly looking ahead, the ship was inconveniently bound to a log and was threatening to sink with everyone on board. All were disturbed and terrified, and they hurriedly strove to bring the ship to shore. When the ship was brought to dry land, those who were inside carried it to the shore, but they forgot the bishop sitting at the stern of the ship. One of the clerics named Mesi, astonished with great amazement, said: "Alas for us miserable ones! for we have not been helpers to our elder in this danger," and having said this, he ran through the depth of the water that had gathered in the ship and, taking the bishop's arms over his shoulders, he lifted him out of the ship. Thus, when all had been exposed and he was the last to exit, the ship sank in the back into the depths. What is surprising if the ship, burdened with him on board, could not sink, but stood upon the water at his command, who by his own will made the waves of the sea firm for the blessed Apostle Peter to walk upon? Thus, it was not due to its own condition, but due to the merits of the one sitting in it that the ship was compelled to float upon the waters until it was relieved of all burdens and cargo, and afterwards it was reported to have sunk.

XVIII. Therefore, when he desired to visit Rome at one time with a burning spirit and reached the river named Tarcum, he found it made so perilous by the flooding of waters that no one from either side of those approaching hoped to be able to come over it that day or another: the holy bishop, trusting in God, hastened to put on his vestments for mass, and on the bank of the river, he devoutly celebrated mass with his companions, and after mass, he crossed the aforementioned river with such ease that none of his companions encountered any adversity, but all went rejoicing along the way, safe and sound, praising God.

XIX. While he fervently insisted on the multimodal services of Christ and sought to amplify them from all sides, by God's grace, he devised a plan to establish a congregation of holy women at the church of Saint Stephen the Protomartyr, named Emoza, to submit to the rule of holiness and to unite those betrothed to Christ God under a holy veil. When this had been accomplished, a certain woman, despising the marriage of her husband with consent, professed herself to be admitted to the same congregation for the reward of future beatitude through obedience, but she did not remain learned in the knowledge of letters, yet she had great zeal for external works of necessity, and thus the other holy women wished to make her the cellarer. When she refused, it was reported to the bishop, and it was requested that the ministry of the cellarer be entrusted to her with his authority. The bishop, assenting to the supplication, commanded that the aforementioned holy woman be made the cellarer; however, she did not obey the bishop's command but tried to persist in her previous refusal. The following night, in a dream, she heard a voice saying to her: "Because you did not obey the command of the bishop, therefore you are deprived of the ability to walk until you are absolved by him." Upon waking, she felt her limbs so weakened that she could not have any effect of walking. Bound by this infirmity, she awaited the bishop's arrival with great labor. Meanwhile, the time for the synodal meeting was approaching, and the bishop was returning to Augusta; when the sick holy woman heard this, she requested to be carried to the church of Saint Mary and to be presented before him, and when she came into his presence, she began to beseech his mercy, that she might be worthy to be absolved from the burdensome bonds of her infirmity. Upon hearing her plea, the bishop rebuked her for her disobedience and dismissed her, granting her both the blessing and the indulgence. When the bishop was returning from her, she was immediately restored to health and ran ahead of the bishop before he had traversed the church, and, prostrating herself before his presence, she praised God for her restored health, promising that she would amend her disobedience henceforth, and she returned joyfully to her own dwelling.

XX. The holy bishop, singing hymns to the Lord, later began to build a church in the cemetery of Saint Mary in the shape of a cross, and, upon completion of the building and the establishment of five altars within it, he dedicated it in honor of Saint John the Baptist, and he had a baptismal font hewn from stone placed in it, and, having legitimized it, he entrusted it to a priest for the administration of divine services, and he commanded that the clerks reverently visit it every Saturday and on other solemn feast days with the Gospel, crosses, and candles, praising God, and in the Paschal week, which they call within the Albas, since it is customary to sing three psalms at Vespers, they should remain there walking and beautifully chanting the remaining two with an antiphon and tone, and he often used to offer saving sacrifices to God there.

XXI. In the last days, Zoam, wishing to save himself, resolved in his mind, although he felt his bodily strength diminishing day by day, to diligently visit the thresholds of the apostles Peter and Paul. And when he had traveled a little distance in a cart and reached more difficult paths, he could not continue the journey further until he began to be carried on a bed placed upon horses: thus, proceeding in this way, although it seemed dangerous to his companions everywhere, with God's help and that of the apostle Saint Peter, he safely reached Rome, fulfilling devoutly the vows and promises he had previously made, and receiving the gifts of most gracious benefits and indulgences, and having been honorably received by Saint Peter and his vicar the pope, and the others serving God there with Saint Peter, he began his happy return and intended to visit Ravenna. As he was approaching there, he learned that the glorious emperor Otto and the empress Adalhaida were staying there, and he sent a messenger ahead to inform them of his arrival, and he immediately followed the messenger to the door of the emperor's chamber. The emperor, when he had learned that he was staying so nearby, hastened to receive him affectionately, one foot shod and the other still unshod, out of humility and the fervor of divine love. And when they were enjoying sweet conversation in the chamber with the summoned empress, and were concluding discussions on various matters alternately, the holy man began to urge the emperor, with the help of the empress, to faithfully and firmly commend to him the care of his sister's son Adalbero's episcopate, and the governance over the household and all secular affairs pertaining to him, and to merit receiving a promise of consolation from his imperial majesty, so that after his departure he might be granted the episcopal seat, allowing him more leisure for the study of prayer, ecclesiastical governance, and the stability of Christianity. The glorious and benevolent emperor, assenting to his request, commended the affairs of the secular business to Adalbero, and promised to grant him the honor of the episcopal seat after the life of the bishop, if God willed, and moreover allowed the bishop to depart lovingly endowed with many pounds of gold, and he cautiously arranged for his residences with other necessary services, with his faithful ones until the end of that province.

XXII. However, the bishop and the aforementioned Adalbero, returning joyfully to the city, were received honorably as was fitting, and all who were found there, having learned of their prosperous return and the honor bestowed upon them by the emperor, were greatly rejoiced. Then the aforementioned Adalbero, gathering the bishop's soldiers, desired that they swear oaths of fidelity to him, which they did in the presence of the bishop; likewise, the household did throughout the entire episcopate. However, the bishop was clothed in garments fashioned in the manner of monks, whose rule he had previously been accustomed to follow in many virtues. And while these things were being done, due to the envy of certain clerics, who thought that after the death of the holy bishop, with the imperial majesty granting it, they could acquire the episcopate, he presumptuously took up the episcopal staff publicly, so that all hope of acquiring the episcopate might be taken away from them.

XXIII. Afterward, when the emperors were returning from Italy, namely the father and his offspring, to France, a synod was held in a place called Ingilunheim, to which the archbishops, along with their other suffragans, honorably invited Saint Ulrich with his legates, and they decided that Adalbero, his nephew, should come with him. When they arrived there, and the bishops gathered there learned that Adalbero was publicly carrying the episcopal staff, they became angry with him, saying that he had fallen into heresy against the rule of canonical rectitude and that he was unjustly claiming the honor of pontifical dignity while the bishop was still alive, and therefore it was not fitting for him to be ordained bishop beyond that. When he heard this, on the first day he avoided entering the synodal discussion and remained in another house with the other clerics of the bishop. However, the bishop entered the synod with a few of his chaplains. And when the pontiffs began to have discussions among themselves, they wished to conclude each matter through the use of the Latin language; and when the cause of Saint Ulrich needed to be addressed, and he, due to illness, could not present his case with such a strong voice that the whole synod could hear, one of his clerics named Gerhard, who was remaining outside the synod with Adalbero, was called to manifest his lord's desire through the use of the Latin language. And when he could scarcely stand in the presence of the emperors and bishops due to the density of the crowd, he was asked what his lord desired. With these questions multiplied, he said: "I cannot respond to your questions on behalf of my lord unless he commands it." To him the bishop said: "Brother, you know well my desire, narrate this, and I beseech you that, with their counsel and permission, may it be fulfilled, with God's help." Then the aforementioned cleric Gerhard said in the presence of all: "Most excellent emperors, and most religious bishops, my lord's desire is to leave the world and to enter a holy life according to the rule of Saint Benedict, and to await the day of his death in a contemplative life. In the clothing of a certain external habit, you can recognize the will of the inner spirit." With these and other reasons presented in his lord's will, he fell to the ground before the feet of the emperors and bishops, beseeching them not to disdain fulfilling his lord's petition according to God's will. They requested a delay in responding until the following day, and afterward deliberated among themselves how the matter of Adalbero would be concluded. Some of the bishops were supporters of Adalbero, so that he would not be entirely excluded from the hope of episcopal ordination after the life of his uncle. While they were conversing among themselves, finally united in one reason, they all affirmed together that unless Adalbero excused himself by oath that he did not know heresy remained because he had taken hold of the episcopal power with the staff, he could in no way be legally made a bishop further. On the following day, the bishop Adalbero also attended the synodal discussion, and, when the aforementioned crime was imputed to him, he resolved to defend himself from the said crime with many objections from various discussions with his supporters. When the assembly of all the bishops did not consent to this, according to the aforementioned destination of the bishops, he completed the oath, in the name of the Father, and the Son, and the Holy Spirit, over the four Gospels. Then again Bishop Ulrich sought responses to his petition, which had been postponed the day before, through his aforementioned cleric, because he desired that his aforementioned nephew should be ordained bishop, and that he, according to the rule of Saint Benedict, should merit to serve in the monastery with their consent. However, the bishops, although they were not entirely pleased with it, did not want to openly contradict his petition in the synod; but the wisest among them, with the counsel of others, asked him to walk outside the synod with them, and there they had a secret conversation with him and his wisest clerics, saying: "Reverend Father, who knows the norm of all ecclesiastical books, who has always walked the path of rectitude without deviating, it is not fitting that now, omitting this way which you have always held, such an error should arise from you, that another should be ordained in your place while you are alive; because if the custom of age begins to be perpetrated from you, in the future many reverend and good bishops, desiring such things from their nephews and clerics, will encounter many adversities. It is better for you to remain in that ministry in which you began to serve God, than, following your own will, to cause scandal to many others; because from you, canons, monks, nuns, and other Christians should be constrained to the state of rectitude, who hasten to fall from themselves through the climates. Those who have fallen carelessly while walking are hoped to be able to be raised up from you, with God's help. Regarding your nephew Adalbero, satisfying your will, we firmly agree that no one else from us, after your departure, should be ordained to that place where you are the pastor, while you are alive, except him." Consenting to these counsels, Saint Bishop Ulrich returned with them to the synod, and then with the consent of the other bishops, he had Adalbero recommended by the emperor in their presence, to have the care of his own and to fulfill the cautious disposition of the entire episcopate in all matters. Thus, when these matters were concluded, the synod ended, and the bishop and Adalbero returned to Augsburg with their own.

XXIV. The aforementioned synod was held in the autumn; and subsequently, with the approach of Easter, after the holy week had ended, the bishop and Adalbero, kindly summoned by Count Rinuvinus [Richuvinus], the son of Dietpald, the bishop's brother, came to the castle named Dilinga to stay there for several days charitably with him and his wife named Hiltegart. Therefore, after a few days had passed, Adalbero had himself bled with a phlebotomist there, and afterwards sat down to dinner with the bishop, and after rising from dinner, laid himself down on the bed to rest. And when everyone had gone to their respective lodgings, that very night Adalbero died suddenly, in the year 973. Herewingus, his priest, when he entered to announce this to the bishop in his chamber, the bishop anticipating his speech, said to him: "Behold, Adalbero has died": To which he replied: "I have entered here to announce this to you; no one else was ahead of me to you, and how could you know this?" To which he replied: "Go, and wake Riuvinus and all who are with us, so that they quickly prepare a vehicle to take his body to the city of Augsburg." The bishop, meanwhile, having sent messengers to Augsburg, commanded that a tomb be prepared in the church of Saint Afra next to his tomb, which was done. He, however, with those who were with him, placed the body in a cart, and, with horses in front, carried it to Augsburg with a large crowd of people. The matricularii, however, with crosses and holy water and candles and incense, and with a great multitude of the household and the other people approaching, met them, and, honorably receiving them, conducted them to the place of the tomb with appropriate prayers and hymns, and there, after the vigils were completed and salutary offerings were made to God for his soul, the bishop, commending the soul to Almighty God, devoutly buried the body. After the commendation of the body was completed, and the bishop returned with sorrow, all returned to their homes with weeping and lamentation and great sadness, because he, having come from a noble lineage, and being handsome, well-versed in the art of grammar, diligent in the service of God, vigorous in good works, eloquent in speech, generous in giving, sorrowful in the adversities of others, enriched with many virtues, swift in aiding the poor, and adorned with manifold kindness, was so quickly laid to rest.

XXV. The religious bishop, having sent a messenger, announced to the emperor the death of his aforementioned nephew and requested that the abbey named Utenbura, which had been granted to him by his imperial authority, be donated to him, not out of greed, but with the intention that he could restore the deliberation that he had previously obtained from the same emperor, which had been written and sealed for the monks serving God there. The emperor granted the abbey through the same messenger and sent great consolation and various forms of health. However, when the messenger returned, he found the bishop in a place called Staphense and narrated the aforementioned events. A few days later, while he was still in the same place, a certain messenger came asking for prayers for the soul of the emperor, and his death was announced to him. From there, as he was returning to Augusta, his nephews came, Count Riuvinus, son of his brother Dietpaldi, and Count Hupaldus, son of his brother Manegoldi, and they asked him to go to the town called Witeselinga and show them the church there, where the bodies of their ancestors had been entrusted to the earth (of which he had often warned them to improve and to enclose the same bodies therein, so that they would no longer be drenched by rain), to arrange it, and to determine how large it should be made. The holy bishop, although he very certainly knew that the separation of his body and soul was near, nevertheless went there for the love of God and for their affection, and with careful planning, he taught them to enlarge that church over the aforementioned bodies, and there he stayed with his nephews for several days, and from there he arrived at the castle named Sunnemotinga, due to the request of Manegoldi, brother of the aforementioned Adalberon. And when they had encamped in the field for grass, near the village called Gerilehona, before they reached there, the sun began to insert its rays of light, and a certain man came who said that Bishop Chunradus had certainly died; and he named the day of his death and the day of his burial. Upon hearing this news, the clerics and other companions were astonished and immediately considered sending a messenger to Augusta, so that the usual prayers for his soul could be fulfilled. To whom the holy bishop, knowing the truth of the matter very certainly, spoke gently, saying: "Do not send a messenger yet; in the morning you will find out how it stands concerning the bishop." The next day, early in the morning, a certain man from Constanzia came and truly contradicted the news of the bishop's death and announced his possibility, according to his custom. However, the holy bishop Ulrichus completed the journey he had begun, and there, as if called to a feast, after the completion of the saving sacrifice which he daily strove to offer to God, although he was greatly weakened in body, he sat daily at the table with the guests, and he did not provide any food for his body except for morsels of bread soaked in water, which he often rejected from his mouth after they had been soaked in water, but he sometimes revived his body with sips of water while still seated at the table. And having completed there the matters for which he had been called, he began to depart; the next day he arrived at a place called Utiuntiga, and there, having summoned the monks from the abbey named Uttenbura, he began to deliberate with them and with his faithful ones how he could restore the deliberation which he had previously obtained from the emperor, as I have mentioned, and he said to them: "Choose one from among you as abbot, who may be useful in the service of God and can be found cautious in your needs. If you choose the one who pleases me for this, I will commend the abbey to him until the presence of my lord the emperor; but if you choose another who does not please me, I will not commend it to him." They replied: "Let your holiness name to us the one who may be pleasing to your authority for the election of our unity." Then he said to them: "I will nominate your brother Rudungum for this ministry." Upon hearing this, the brothers asked for a respite until they could all speak together to see if this election could be made with the consent of all the brothers. And when the brothers, gathered in the designated place, began to have discussions among themselves about the aforementioned election, some brothers were pleased, some displeased, but nevertheless, strengthened by the counsel of friends, they united in the will of the bishop and elected Rudungum as abbot, and, returning with him to the bishop, they announced to him their election of unity. Upon hearing this, the bishop, taking his staff, commended the abbey to the aforementioned Rudungum until the presence of the emperor, who at that time had succeeded his father in the empire, and he commended him to his nephews and other faithful ones, so that they might present him to the highness of the emperor, and with their faith assisting him, these might be confirmed by him. When these matters were thus fulfilled, he returned to his own episcopal seat.

XXVI. Upon entering the walls of the city of Augusta, he was seized with great sadness for the death of his grandson Adalberon and for the passing of the emperor, to whom he had always remained faithful in all things, and whose love was firmly glued to his heart. For the rest of the souls of both, he generously distributed many alms to the poor and poured forth many prayers and supplications to the Lord daily, that He might deign to have mercy on them. He did not cease to celebrate the offices of the Mass daily until his bodily strength was so diminished that he could no longer stand by himself. At the table, he sat and held a feast with those who were seated with him, and he, as if fasting, refrained from eating. Afterwards, in the church or in his chamber, he was refreshed by the sweet singing of psalms or by listening to sacred readings. When his bodily strength had so failed him that he could not sing the Mass by himself, he was devoutly brought into the church daily to hear it and did not cease to engage in prayer during that time. For certain, after the Mass was completed, when he entered his chamber, he did not commend himself to the rest of the bed before the evening hour, but sat shod on his seat, and sometimes leaned over to the right on a cushion, sometimes to the left, and sometimes sitting, leaned back against the rear of the seat on which he sat. And after completing the course of the entire psalter, he listened to the sacred readings of the books read by Gerhard, the prior [perhaps of the cathedral], and sometimes enjoyed sweet conversation with him. When a certain conversation among them had ended, the aforementioned cleric asked him, saying: "Do you have hope in this illness, Lord, that your death is imminent?" To which he, as if rebuking him, replied: "Why have you said this? I do not hope, but I certainly know that the day of my death will come to me not many days from now." Concerning this matter, the priest, saddened, sought forgiveness and said to him: "Lord, whom do you command to call for the commendation of your body?" To which he replied: "At the time when my soul shall leave this body, you cannot summon any of them here: because my fellow provincial Bishop Chunradus is so detained by illness that he cannot come here, and the bishops of Bavaria have gathered in France for a royal council." Then he said: "Lord, what should we do then?" To which the holy bishop said: "Do you know how to commend a man's body to the earth?" And he said: "If such a person were to whom our commendation should be made, we would have no fear from that." To which the bishop said: "Do what you can about this matter when the time comes; the Lord will provide a commender for my body." And having said this, the aforementioned priest took up the use of reading again, and in it, as he was accustomed, until the sound of the evening praise hour was announced. The readings were from the Lives of the Holy Fathers and the book of Saint Gregory, which is called the Dialogues; the last book of which discusses much about those who were raptured from the body in spirit and saw many things, and then returned to the body. Thus, conversing in this way, he awaited the day of his death most beautifully, and sometimes saw many things in spirit, of which he narrated a few to those who were with him. Meanwhile, to Abbot Werinharius of the aforementioned monastery of Vulta [Fulda], who came to him for a visitation, he said among other things: "You should become bishop here after me; all have chosen you except for two, and if those two had agreed with the others, your election would undoubtedly have been perfect." And having said this, he grasped the hands of Attelin, the vice lord, and the hands of Hiltin, the chamberlain, commending them to his fidelity, and permitted him to depart with love.

XXVII. On another occasion, one day, as if awakened from a deep sleep, he said to those present listening to him: "Alas! alas! that I ever saw my grandson Adalbero, because since I consented to his desires, they do not want to receive me into their company unpunished!" And having said this, he immediately fell silent. Indeed, the strength of his body was decreasing day by day, to such an extent that he could not enter the church unless supported by two men. However, on the feast day of Saints Mark and Marcellinus, which is the 14th of the Kalends of July, he was brought into the church to hear Mass. After the Mass was completed, he ordered a rug to be laid down at the Holy Cross and prostrated himself upon it. There, having lain for almost half an hour, he rose and summoned the chamberlain, Presbyter Liutpald, to come to him, and he commanded him to bring all his belongings that he had in service before him and to place them before the altar, except for one set of household items and one covering for the table, which he left for the service of his successor. When they had been placed before him and he had seen them, he said: "What should all these things mean to me now?" Although they seemed many to him, their number was no more than a few shirts, seven or eight tablecloths, two blankets, and ten solidi of silver, which he immediately entrusted to the hand of Gerhard the provost to be given to the poor. Moreover, he arranged for all the other items to be divided among the clerics of the same place. From his garments, he sent to the venerable man Antonio, whom he had previously enclosed at Utenburam in the name of God. He also sent clothing to a certain Ruozoni, who was unable to move his limbs except for his arms, and who had a dwelling in the cemetery of the monastery of Campidona, built like a bed raised from the ground, so that the clothing he had worn could be separated from his dwelling by falling to the ground; for previously, when the bishop resided in the same monastery, he often visited the aforementioned poor man himself and gladly listened to the sweetness of his speech, because the same poor man always remained in praises and prayers to God day and night with a closed door. O what tongue can narrate a man of such kindness, who, placed at the end of his life, did not cease to clothe Christ with such a space of time intervening! Certainly because he was always present to him who wanted his members to be clothed by him. After these matters were arranged, he commanded the vice-count and others whom he wished among his faithful and ministers to divide everything found in all places pertaining to his service into three parts, and that one third should be given immediately to the presbyters and the poor with prudent distribution while he was still alive; and this was done. For certain, although his body was held by a grave illness, his senses, spirit, and will could not be occupied, except [so that they did not] insist on pious intentions.

XXVII. On another occasion, one day, as if awakened from a deep sleep, he said to those present and listening: "Alas! alas! that I ever saw my grandson Adalberon, because for the sake of agreeing with him according to his desire, they do not want to receive me into their company without punishment!" And having said this, he immediately fell silent. Indeed, the strength of his body was diminishing day by day, to such an extent that he could not enter the church unless supported by two people. However, on the feast day of Saints Mark and Marcellinus, which is the 14th day before the Kalends of July, he was brought into the church to hear Mass, and after the Mass was completed, he ordered a tapestry to be laid down for him at the Holy Cross, and he prostrated himself upon it. There, having lain for almost half an hour, he rose and summoned the chamberlain Liutpald, the priest, to come to him, and he commanded that all his belongings which the latter had in his ministry be brought into his presence and placed before the altar, except for one preparation for the house and tables, and one mardrin covering which he left for the service of his successor. When these were placed before him and he had seen them, he said: "What were all these things to me now?" Although they seemed numerous to him, their number was no greater than a few shirts, and seven or eight tables, and two cushions, and ten solidi of silver, which he immediately entrusted to the hand of Gerhard, the provost, to be distributed to the poor. All the remaining items he arranged to be divided among the clerics of that place. From his garments, he sent to the venerable man Antonio, whom he had previously enclosed at Utenburam in the name of God. He also transmitted clothing to a certain Ruozon, who was lacking mobility in his limbs, except for his arms, and whose dwelling was built in the cemetery of the monastery of Campidona, raised above the ground like a bed, so that the items which had been arranged by him might be separated from the dwelling by falling to the ground; because previously, when the bishop resided in the same monastery, he often visited the aforementioned poor man himself, and gladly listened to the sweetness of his speech, for this same poor man always remained in praises and prayers to God day and night with the door closed. O what tongue can narrate a man of such kindness, who, placed at the end, did not cease to clothe Christ with such a wide interval in between! Certainly because he was always present to him who wanted to be clothed by him. Having arranged these matters, he commanded the vicedominus and others whom he wished among his faithful and ministers to divide everything found in all places pertaining to his service into three parts, and that one-third should be immediately given to the priests and the poor with careful distribution while he was still alive; which was done. For certain, although the body had been held by a severe illness, the senses, spirit, and will could not be occupied, except to pursue pious intentions.

XXVIII. Therefore, on the holy day of the Nativity of Saint John the Baptist, at the first hour of the day, as if suddenly awakened from sleep, blessed Ulrich said to his attendants: "Put on my garments and shoes." They hesitated because of his great illness, unsure whether he was commanding this in a state of ecstasy or due to incapacity of senses; nevertheless, fulfilling his command, they dressed him in his garments and shoes. Immediately, he ordered that the preparation for the Mass be put on him; and when he was ready, he walked through the main church and reached the church of Saint John the Baptist, which he had previously built and consecrated in his honor, and there he powerfully and carefully celebrated the Mass, which he was accustomed to sing in the early morning for the anniversary solemnities; and when it was finished, he immediately began the public Mass, and with God's help, he completed it most devoutly. Both Masses, as he brought to a conclusion standing without the assistance of others, with blessings, he sat down, and said to the clerics standing by him: "These mysteries which I have now completed by God's grace, I did not assume from the capacity of my body, but by command: for today, while I lay in bed as if asleep, two young men of most beautiful appearance stood before my bed, one of whom said to me: 'Why do you not rise? For you must celebrate Mass today for Saint John the Baptist.' To which the other replied: 'How can this be done, since due to the impossibility of the body, he has not yet completed the first?' But the one who spoke to me before said: 'Rise and hasten to fulfill the mystery of God in the aforementioned church, for today, besides you, no one else will celebrate Mass there.' After saying this, he returned to the chamber. And while he awaited the day of his death with a devoted mind and joyful heart, according to the words of the psalmist David saying: As the deer longs for the springs of water, so my soul longs for you, O God (Psalm 41), although he did not speak in words, he nevertheless manifested in deeds that he believed he would depart from this world on the vigil of the apostles Peter and Paul. On the same day, before the evening praise began, and while all the bells were being rung together by the guardians, having bathed and dressed in the preparation he had kept for his death, he laid himself down as if to die. When the evening praise was finished, with others helping him, he raised himself from the ground and said quietly: "O Saint Peter, you have not done as I expected!" And he remained somewhat troubled in mind about this matter. The aforementioned priest Gerhard said to him: "Lord, do not be saddened, but remember that it similarly happened to other holy bishops; for it was said to one: 'On the feast of the apostles, you will be brought to rest from this world,' and he, hoping to die on the feast of the apostles, was delayed until the eighth day, and then he died. To Bishop Cassius of Narni, it was said by a certain priest, beaten by an angel: 'Your hand shall not cease, your foot shall not cease, do what you are doing, work what you are working, you will come to me on the feast of the apostles.' But the bishop, thinking his death was imminent on the solemnity of the apostles, which was then approaching, sought in every way to prepare for the deposition of his body. Therefore, when the solemnity was approaching, he remained healthy and whole, and thus he remained until seven years had passed, and then on the same day, as he had been told, after many good things had been done and the sacred ministry fulfilled, he happily departed from this world." Having heard this, the holy bishop remembered it to be true and answered him, saying: "You have spoken well, brother," and he remained uplifted in spirit and with good cheer, and he showed himself sweet and agreeable to those remaining with him: rebuking no one, scolding no one, angry with no one, troublesome to no one, no word of lamentation was heard from him, but he did all the good he could at that time, for those present and absent. The aforementioned Count Richwin, his nephew, was still not returning from royal business. Of him, he sometimes said: "O Richwin, would that you would come while I am alive so that I could see you!" That year, the solemnity of the apostles Peter and Paul fell on Sunday, which he awaited with the best intentions, as I have said, until the day of Thursday had passed; on that night, before dawn of Friday could be well known, having sprinkled himself with ashes in the shape of a cross and sprinkled with holy water, he made himself lie down, and thus he lay until dawn illuminated the entire breadth of the world. Then Richwin, returning from the palace, entered and recited the emperor's message while he was listening. Upon seeing him and hearing the message, he raised his eyes and, according to his ability, gave thanks to Almighty God who, according to the words of the prophet David: "He will fulfill the desire of those who fear him," etc. (Psalm 145.) When Richwin had departed, at that same hour, while the clerics were devoutly singing the litany, commending his soul to God, in the year of the incarnation of our Lord Jesus Christ 973, at the age of 83, on the 4th day of July, the 4th of that month, on Friday, he peacefully passed away as if in sweet sleep, freed from the prison of the body, and departed to rest. For certain, when the holy body had been stripped for washing in the usual manner, it filled the nostrils of all those remaining there with a sweet fragrance, and it remained so until the body was washed, clothed in the appointed garments, and placed on the bier, to be carried into the church. Indeed, when the clergy heard that the bishops of Bavaria were returning from the aforementioned meeting to their province, they sent a messenger to summon Archbishop Frederick for the commendation of the sacred body; and when the messenger came to him, he found him so detained by a great fever that he could not come. But when the messenger returned with sadness, he heard that the venerable Bishop Wolfgang had wished to come to a place called Nordilinga; he hurried to meet him. When he certainly arrived, greeted by him, he heard that he wished to go to Augsburg to visit the holy servant of God Ulrich, detained by illness. To him, he replied: "The Lord has commanded your holiness to visit him, and I have come to announce to you that he has died, and to urge you from all the congregation there serving God, to hasten to come and commend the holy body to God." Upon hearing this, the holy bishop was enveloped in great sorrow; on that same night, he rose at dawn and began to go to Augsburg. However, on the journey, when he realized that he could not arrive there at an appropriate time, he sent the same messenger ahead to announce his arrival. Meanwhile, the body was being carefully and devoutly guarded day and night by the congregation in the church of Saint Mary with prayers and celebrations of Mass until the day of Sunday. On Sunday, after the first Mass celebrated for his soul, when the clergy and the congregation of nuns had gathered, and a great multitude of people from the provinces had arrived, the priests lifted the body and began to carry it to Saint Afra, where his tomb had been prepared beforehand. When they came to the hill called Pereleich, the aforementioned messenger arrived and announced the arrival of Bishop Wolfgang. However, they, carrying the body into the church of Saint Afra, also celebrated the sacrificial Mass with all devotion for the rest of his soul. But since the bishop had still not arrived, and the hour of the day was not delayed, unless the time for the public celebration of God's ministry was imminent, and this was to be performed with all devotion by the congregation of clerics, the aforementioned bishop came, who, having been honorably received, and having concluded the prayer, greeted the brothers and said: "What do you think, shall we commend the sacred body today, or shall we postpone it to another day?" To which the brothers responded, saying: "If it pleases your holiness, it seems good to us if it is announced to all who are now present that they gather here at the appropriate hour tomorrow for the commendation of the sacred body, and that a gift of the saving host may be offered to God by us sacrificing for the rest of his soul, for the appropriate hour has passed, and you are weighed down with great fatigue." Upon hearing this, the bishop, gladly assenting to their counsel, awaited another day. That night, Hiltegart, the wife of the aforementioned Count Richwin, although married, was still quite religious, came and brought a linen cloth soaked in wax, and asked the highest clerics to carefully and secretly wrap it around the sacred body, lest the priestly garment, in which he was clad, should soon be consumed by the earth, because he himself, while still alive, commanded that they should not place a wooden board under his body, but let them lay pure earth and cover it with a wooden lid: who, according to his petition, wrapped the linen cloth around the sacred body. In the morning, when a great multitude of people arrived, and clerics and nuns gathered there serving God, as well as many from the provinces, joining in sacred offices, the bishop, offering the saving host to God with great contrition of heart and humility for the rest of his soul, also completed the public Mass, and admonished all in common with sober and careful speech, that for that holy soul they should pray with deep intention of heart devoutly, that, being freed from all bonds of sins, by God's grace, she might be worthy to enjoy eternal joy with the saints and chosen ones of God. After the prayer according to his word was completed by all, the bishop buried the body and most devoutly commended the soul to Almighty God with tears. The ministers, as has been said, covered the body with a wooden lid, and over this they placed a dense wooden flooring on the steps of the walled tomb, and firmly closed it on the surface of the earth with joined stones. When these things were thus completed, the bishop went to Augsburg for the sake of prayer. After many prayers had been completed, he was asked by the brothers through charity to take on the preparation for the Mass, which belonged to Saint Ulrich, of which abundance he had while living, for his holiness: and honorably, as he was most worthy, he was dismissed and returned to his own, accompanied by God.

XXVIII. After the death of Saint Ulrich, bishop, Heinrich, the son of Purchard, became his successor, not by entering the sheepfold wisely, but by ascending from another place, because with the counsel of Purchard, the leader of the Alamanni, who had his aunt's daughter as his wife, and many others, as well as certain knights who cunningly wished to increase their benefits from him, he began to consider with subtle counsel how he might usurp the aforementioned position for himself; although it came to his knowledge that Abbot Werinharius, in a certain invisible gathering of the carnal eyes, where Saint Ulrich was in an ecstasy of mind, heard: If two were to agree with each other, he would have been destined from that entire congregation for this ministry, to become his successor, as I have previously predicted. Certain clerics, accompanied by some knights from the same episcopate, began to journey to the court of the emperor bearing the episcopal staff. And when they came to the city of Worms to the monastery of Saint Cyriacus, they found Purchard, the duke, occupied with illness along with his wife. When they indicated to him their intention of their journey, they were cunningly deceived by certain machinations from him; for he told them that the emperor was staying near the farthest borders of his kingdom these days, and that on the road they were to take, everything was excessively barren, and the grass remained everywhere in defense, and therefore they themselves and their horses could not be sustained with any convenience. Not many days later, our emperor wished to hold a royal council at a place called Erinstein; you can easily go there, therefore return now, and when my certain messenger arrives to announce to you the day of the aforementioned speech, do not hesitate to come there; for there you will find me to be a firm helper for you, and in the episcopal election know that I will be in agreement with you without ambiguity. Upon hearing these words, considering them to be true and consenting to his counsel, they returned. However, not long after, the duke's messenger came and indicated that the royal council was to remain at the aforementioned place, and he admonished them to come there. They immediately hastened to the aforementioned place, taking other brothers with them. And when they approached the place called Balneos, a certain messenger met them and said: "Heinrich, the son of Purchard, whom the emperor and Duke Purchard have decided to be bishop at Augsburg, will soon meet you." Upon hearing this, the brothers, saddened that they had to be deprived of the aforementioned election of the bishop, did not advance further, but returned to a suitable place to wait until they could accompany the aforementioned Heinrich. On that same day, when the soldiers who came from Duke Purchard with Heinrich arrived at the camp, they began to ask the clerics accompanying them to confirm Heinrich as bishop in common at that same place. They requested a truce until all the brothers at home could gather together. And when the soldiers refused this and contended with long discourse among themselves, they returned to Heinrich, and with certain clerics they elected him to be bishop over them; however, some who did not elect him went to Augsburg to the other brothers. And when they arrived at Augsburg, thus separated in his election, a certain count named Wolverad came with some other men, as if bringing a delegation from the emperor to the congregation, saying: "The emperor has demanded grace and mercy and all good things from you, and has requested that you unanimously do not refuse to elect this lord Heinrich, whom he has decided to be your pastor at this place, out of love for him." But this delegation was composed of a fraudulent scheme. To whom they responded: "Let him come with you to our chapter to hear our responses." And when they could barely obtain permission to enter the chapter, they were reading canonical lessons on the election of bishops. The aforementioned Heinrich, having heard that in the recited lessons it was in the power of the canons to elect or reject him, humbly requested that they would not disdain to elect him as bishop, promising them that if they consented to his request, he would in the future provide for all kinds of convenience. Believing his promises, some voluntarily, some avoiding disputes, nonetheless all together decided that he should be bishop. This election, when it became known in the church among the soldiers and household, was confirmed by the ringing of bells from all. Then finally the aforementioned Heinrich, having taken some canons with him, went to the emperor and, in his presence, supported by the testimony of others, announced his election, humbly begging that from the height of his imperial power the aforementioned pontificate would be granted to him. However, the emperor did not contradict his petition, nor did he fulfill it immediately, but promised that after five days at the solemnity of Saint Mauritius he would grant assent to his petition, as he did. Later, at the appointed time, he came to Mainz and received episcopal blessing from Archbishop Rudpert and his suffragans. At that time Otto, the son of Luitolf, the son of Emperor Otto, was duke of the Alamanni, and Heinrich, the son of Heinrich, his brother, was duke of the Bavarians: who, although they should have been united in love by close kinship, began to exercise envy and dissension among themselves by the machination of the evil instigator Satan. Therefore, Heinrich the bishop remained more suitable to his duke in all things, and was more consenting to his counsels than to Duke Otto, although the city of Augsburg remained situated in his duchy. For this reason, Duke Otto began to be angry against him, and with his faithful began to take counsel on how he might oppose him in whatever ways he could; which he did. Moreover, the bishop wished to withdraw benefits from certain soldiers, nephews of Saint Bishop Ulrich, Manegold and Hulpald, because of certain counsels, without their guilt. They, however, because they had often come to the aid of the emperor sent by Bishop Saint Ulrich while he was still alive, and fulfilling his will vigorously in all things, remained until they were honored with gifts through his grace and were dismissed to return. The queen also professed to be a relative of theirs; therefore, having received benefits, they opposed the bishop and kept them in their power, against his will. Therefore, the bishop, wearied by these and many other adversities, became sad. At one time, when Emperor Otto wished to invade the Slavic people with an army, and Otto, who was then duke of the Alamanni and Bavarians, was prepared to come to his aid with the Alamanni and Noricans, Heinrich the bishop promised to go with him, waited with his soldiers until the army withdrew, and, as they had previously counseled, he occupied the cities he could with his soldiers, and he himself entered Nuwingburg. However, Heinrich, who had previously been duke, entered the city of Pazon, intending that, as Otto was withdrawing with the army, he would subjugate the province with the aid of his nephew the bishop. When this plan became known to Duke Otto, he returned with the army of both provinces and besieged him in the aforementioned city, Pazova. However, Emperor Otto, having been delivered from the Slavs by God's mercy, came after him to that same city in his siege. And when the siege was over and the situation calmed, as the emperor was returning to Saxony, after a set time Heinrich, the son of Heinrich, and his counterpart, the son of Perhtolf, were summoned to the emperor's council, with whom also Heinrich the bishop came to the emperor to excuse himself for the aforementioned guilt, so that he might be deemed worthy to return to his own by his grace restored. After the council was completed, Heinrich and his counterpart were sent into exile. However, Heinrich the bishop was entrusted to Wurdina, where Saint Luitger rests, to be kept. And when he was being guarded there with great caution from Easter until after the nativity of Saint John the Baptist, an imperial council was held in a town called Trulmanna. There came two presbyters, Gerhard and Anamotus, from Augsburg, and, with the intervention of Duke Otto and the bishops found there, they pleaded not only for themselves but for all clerics and laypeople living in that same episcopate, that they not be deprived of episcopal custody for long. However, the emperor, satisfying the petition of Duke Otto and of his other faithful and the clerics present, commanded that the bishop be brought back from exile, and in his presence, again granting him the oath of fidelity, allowed him to return to his episcopate with his grace. Restored to his place, the bishop began to consider in his mind for what offenses such diverse adversities had frequently befallen him, who was insulted by the duke in many ways more than his predecessors; and because the leaders of the soldiers presumed to have their benefits against his will, and the most chosen ministers from his paternal family had suddenly perished in various ways, he secretly asked his familiar clerics if Saint Ulrich had said about Abbot Werinharius that he should become his successor, as had been said to him before. And when he had come to know the truth, which he had previously refused to believe, he was greatly frightened, but did not publicly manifest it; he was more frightened because at that time frequently great and marvelous signs were occurring at the tomb of Saint Bishop Ulrich, through God's granting. Then finally, changed in many ways for the better, he attempted to reconcile himself with God, and commanded that the mother church be covered with a new roof, and he built a bridge over the river Licus at Saint Afra. And, so that none from the family should receive tolls or any payment from the bridge, he commanded that anyone who wished should go there for his alms without contradiction and occupation. Later, he also visited Rome and the thresholds of the holy apostles Peter and Paul for the remission of his sins. And before he began to go there, he transferred the property which his father Purchard seemed to have in Geisinhaus, and which he had entrusted to his faithful Ethicho under testimony, namely so that he would firmly transfer it there, where his son Heinrich the bishop would request it, then for certain, at the request of Ethicho, he delivered the aforementioned property legally into his hand, according to the law of the Noricans, situated at the altar of Saint Mary in the city of Augsburg, and upon the gilded chest decorated with stones, with the church and all buildings, with fields, meadows, pastures, mills, waters and watercourses, roads and paths, cities, woods, mown and unmown, sought and still to be sought, and with the household and with all that pertains to the same property by right, except for twenty hubas he left outside the transfer; and he decreed that they be assigned to the service of Saint Magnus at Fauces; he arranged with the canons that they would have the power, if they wished, to exchange the same twenty hubas with ten located in a good place in this province, into the hands of Werinharius the advocate, and into the hands of Gerhard the provost, for the remedy of his soul, and of his father, mother, and aunt, and of other relatives and kin, in such a way that it remains in the law and power of the canons perpetually in offering, saving in all their daily stipend; and that they, for the repose of his soul, annually before the anniversary day at evening hour should celebrate a full vigil of voice, and on the anniversary day again complete the vigil, and after the mass of the altar, all should offer the oblation of the victims to God in common, and moreover should provide for one hundred poor people with sufficient stipend for eating and drinking, and from them should clothe twelve, in one year with woolen garments, and in another year should clothe them with linen, and should provide shoes and footwear. But if any successor of his bishop should attempt to break this agreement, and by removing the aforementioned property from the canons for his own benefit should attempt to restore it in any way, and thus upon being discovered does not restore it immediately, his legitimate heirs shall have the free power to place three denarii upon the altar, and redeem the same property from there and possess it in their own right for all future generations.

Written at Augusta, in the church of Saint Mary, Mother of God, before the altar, carried out by Bishop Heinrich, in the presence of the canons, before a multitude of people and before the witnesses noted below.

+ Signed by Etih who made this tradition.
+ Signed by Adalbero.
+ Signed by Jagob.

This work was produced in association with:

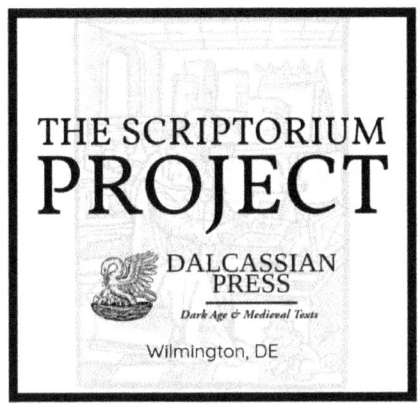

www.ingramcontent.com/pod-product-compliance
Lightning Source LLC
LaVergne TN
LVHW061048070526
838201LV00074B/5226